FOREWOR

This year the Frome Yearbook celebrates its 35th a
have been produced. In 1987, the first year of pub
McGarvie, the society chairman, Laurie Bowring ex
had been published since the society's foundation in
ambitious product. Today the society is on a sound ɪɪɪɑɪɪₐ ......ɡ
membership of over 460 members and able to produce a journal which it is hoped will find a
readership beyond the confines of the town.

Although this is only my second issue I have been delighted by the volume and quality of the
material that has been submitted by members and non-members. Please continue to research,
write and contribute to what could become an important contribution to the recording of
Frome's illustrious past and help to safeguard its attractions for those who come after us.

Life has changed in a great many ways since 1987 and perhaps the biggest change has been
the introduction of the internet which has improved and speeded up research and recording in
ways unimaginable 35 years ago. It has enabled us to reach a much wider audience with our
own website and it has also enabled us to reproduce many monographs and Yearbooks some
long out of print and unobtainable. A selection of these are being scanned and made available
to anyone interested in the town's history, downloadable in PDF format from either the society
website, www.fsls.org.uk or the museum, www.frome-heritage-museum.org without charge
saving a considerable amount of research from oblivion. We have also greatly expanded the
range of publications on Frome and its villages which are available to purchase from the
Society or in person from the museum, the full list is downloadable from the websites.

In terms of future publications, the big event of the coming year will be our atlas of the 1813
Jeremiah Cruse map of Frome Selwood Parish, due out in early 2023 to be accompanied by
an exhibition at the museum, with which the society is developing an increasingly close
working relationship. We have acquired the rights to the best-selling *Historic Inns of Frome*
which will be reprinted this year and a number of other books are in preparation including a
new anthology of the town's major events, characters and unique aspects.

In other spheres there is a new series of town walks in conjunction with the Town Council
which encompasses an ever-expanding range of topics from local celebrities like Christina
Rossetti and Sir Benjamin Baker to our precious listed buildings which include the
Blue House and the ancient houses of Gentle Street and Rook Lane. There are a number of
themed walks throughout the warmer months such as Saxon Frome and Frome the War Years.

Our programme of coach trips and lectures continues to delight and is heavily
subscribed; again, a full list can be seen on our website.

The Civic Society, which is incorporated with Frome Society is another important part of our
work and welcomes those with experience in planning, development and conservation to
help us ensure that the inevitable expansion of Frome will both preserve and enhance its
unique character.

Mick Davis, Editor.

A
MAP
OF
THE PARISH OF
FROME SELWOOD
in the County of
SOMERSET

CELEBRATING FROME'S HIDDEN MASTERPIECE

The Jeremiah Cruse Map of the Parish of Frome Selwood, 1813

Dr Pat Smith

For all of us who love local history, archives are treasure troves; and few documents are more exciting than original, hand-drawn maps. So it was with great anticipation that a small research team from the Frome Society visited the Somerset Heritage Centre (SHC) last September to examine Jeremiah Cruse's 1813 map of Frome Selwood parish.

The initial impression of the map is its sheer size: 11 feet 5 inches (3.47m) high by 6 feet 6 inches (2.1m) wide. The scale (in chains) is the equivalent of 20 inches to a mile, with grid squares being a scant 5 inches. The whole map covers 4 miles by 6.7 miles and is orientated with north set 38% to the right of the vertical. Its full extent is shown on the facing page with some details appearing on the front cover of this Yearbook.

The Society's research team were joined by Dr Adrian Webb, an expert in historic maps, to advise on the map's physical state and authenticity. He confirmed that the materials, drawing style and colouration were all consistent with an early 19th century production and indeed with Jeremiah Cruse's work. The map, hand drawn and coloured on paper, is backed by three joined vertical strips of linen, measuring 681mm, 731mm and 714mm respectively. The colours are well preserved and the overall condition is good, with little damage other than worn edges. There is a pole at the bottom; that at the top is missing.

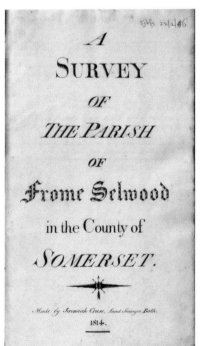

The map includes over 3,000 individually marked plots of land. The key to these landholdings is in a Survey Book, also known as a terrier, (*title page, left*) a handwritten tabular index to all the plots numbered on the map, their descriptions, size, cultivation, owners and occupiers in 1814. This book is held in the archives of St John's Church Frome, for which it was originally commissioned. It is, in itself, a remarkable piece of documentary history; combined with the map, it opens a unique window onto early 18th century Frome.

The map was donated to the Frome Society in 1965. and in 1975, Michael McGarvie lodged some photocopies with the SHC, but the map itself remained at the house (and makeshift museum), bequeathed to the Society by Katherine Ashworth. When the Society sold the house in 1984, the map was passed to the SHC, where it is held on behalf of Frome Museum.

This important heritage asset has therefore been archived away for some 40 years and, although it is on open access, very few people have been aware of its existence.

In the past, there seems to have been understandable confusion between the St John's map now held at the SHC and a very similar map made by Jeremiah Cruse for the Marquess of Bath, also in 1813, to the same size and scale. This is held in the archives at Longleat, catalogued as: *A Map of the Parish of Frome Selwood in the County of Somerset'. Surveyed by Jeremiah Cruse, Land Surveyor of Bath.* The Longleat map recorded the Marquess's extensive landholdings in Frome, with 'lands in a state of tillage coloured yellow, meadow and pasture green, and lands belonging to the Vicarage of Frome, purple'. Other plots were uncoloured. There is a corresponding survey book for the Longleat map, dated 1813 (there is a microfilm copy at the SHC).

The question arises as to why there would be a second version of this very large and expensively produced map and survey book. This might have remained a mystery, if someone had not scribbled, on a page towards the end of the Longleat survey book, this note:

The Present Map with Copy of the Terrier and additional Reference to Richardson's Map lowest sum - ['£200' crossed out] £150. This is fairly worth to the Parish of Frome £500. Or, to give a Copy of the Reference reduced into form with each Proprietors Lands brought into a Total for £220'.

The St John's version of the Terrier has indeed an additional column cross-referencing Cruse's plot numbers with 'numbers on Mr R's map': i.e. Richard Richardson's 1799 survey of Frome (also held at Longleat). Evidently the Church requested and accepted the quotation, the second map was swiftly produced, still carrying the date 1813, followed by the second Survey Book with plot details for 1814. Although £150 would be the equivalent of at least £10,000 today, this would certainly have been 'fairly worth' the cost and more, for it gave the Church a complete overview of landholdings in the Parish of Frome and Selwood, for the purpose of raising church rates, tithes and other income.

Having confidently established the origins and provenance of the map, the Society now intends to make it available to a wider public by producing a limited edition, in atlas form, in early 2023. This will faithfully reproduce, in over 100 full colour plates, the entire map at its original scale.

We will be offering the atlas initially by subscription to those who wish to secure their copy. A full transcription of the Survey book will be included in advance of publication, and Society members will be given priority when the scheme is launched in September 2022.

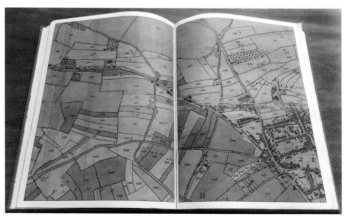

Above: artist's impression of the Atlas.

WILLIAM WALTER WHEATLEY

Part I Tracing an Artist

Mick Davis

WW Wheatley was a watercolourist famous locally for his depictions of the streets, churches and antiquities of Frome and surrounding villages. His origins, and much of his life, has been shrouded in mystery and this article is an attempt to pull together details that have been discovered by past researchers and add recent research. It concentrates on his personal and family life rather than his standing as an artist; he surely deserves a full biography but much more research needs to be done.

Wheatley is generally recorded as having been born in Bristol in 1811 but his own estimates as to his date of birth taken from the census returns range from 1804 to 1811 and it is the latter, from the 1881 census, which appears on his death certificate giving his age at death as 74. All census entries agree that he was born in Weymouth and research by his great great grandson, David Friend, has revealed that he was baptised in Melcombe Regis (Weymouth) on 22 of August 1802 the son of John Francis Wheatley and his wife Mary. (Melcombe Regis baptism records.) A search of the parish registers revealed that there was no family called Wheatley in the town at that time indicating that their origins lie elsewhere.

Much of the information about his background is contained in a series of letters from Mr Friend in New Zealand to Michael McGarvie in Frome. Friend died before they had a chance to examine the evidence together. His letters contain a mixture of solid research and conjecture and it is sometimes hard to distinguish between the two but worth going through them in summary to assist future researchers. The originals are in Frome Museum.

When William Wheatley married in 1859 the marriage certificate gave his father as 'John Wheatley officer in the 66th Regiment, deceased.' No further mention of a John *Francis* Wheatley has been traced. A John Wheatley, married Mary Banbury at Exeter St David's on 11 November 1785, he is described as a soldier and Mary as a spinster who had been baptised at Ilfracombe in 1772. If baptised shortly after birth this would have made her 13 at the time of the marriage which was legal with the consent of the parents but it is also possible that her baptism took place some years after her birth.

The career of this John Wheatley has been traced in part as an Ensign/Lieutenant in the Royal West Middlesex Militia in 1809 followed by the 38th Regiment of Foot (Staffordshire's) through various battles in the Peninsula Wars until his death at the battle of San Sebastian on 31 August 1813 when William would have been about 11. There is no trace of any children before the baptism of William in 1802, 17 years after their marriage which is strange. Is this the same John that married Mary Banbury in 1785? If so it is curious that he had only attained the rank of ensign despite being in the army for at least 24 years. Friend is almost convinced that they are the same and father to William, but despite much further research nothing has been discovered to link the two beyond doubt. We are missing a vital piece of evidence such as a place of birth, date of birth, mention of a wife, family home, anything however small that could link him (or them) to William. If there are two separate John Wheatleys are either of them the father of William?

Following Friend's retelling of family tradition, he states that, William's siblings were John Francis Wheatley who was born on 16 December 1804 and baptised at the parish church of St Andrew, Stoke Damerel on the 24th. This entry has been found and it is very encouraging that the child was given the same name as the one on William's baptism entry, although on this occasion the father gives his name as simply' John'! He is said to have taken off to Drury Lane at an early age first becoming an actor, then a musician and at his death in the Wincanton poorhouse he was described as a juggler. Nothing has been discovered to confirm this life story.

Another brother was Ernest who according to family tradition became a non-commissioned officer in an infantry regiment and later the marines. Strangely, there was an Ernest Adolphus son of John & Mary Wheatley baptised at Stoke Damerel on 22 February 1807 but he died at the age of one year and three months and was buried on 29 April 1808. Any trace of a later son named Ernest has yet to be found.

Daughter Amelia Wheatley, married Henry Tilbury a seaman from HMS *Scorpion* at Stoke Damerel on 11 April 1810. Immediately afterwards a William Davidson of the same ship was married followed by a number of other seamen from different ships over the following days. Her baptism has not been traced but she would have been the eldest, born in around 1789 or before if she was of full age at her marriage.

Going back further a John Wheatley was buried in the church in 1703 and there are a number of other mentions of the name in the area making it highly likely that Stoke Damerel was the home of the Wheatley family. The fate of Mary Wheatley has not been discovered but if she had died at a relatively early age it would give further credence to the idea that William did not know the year of his birth. Amelia was a lot older than William and John Francis so perhaps she took charge of the family once their parents had died. It is believed that his early years were spent between Stoke Damerel, Ilfracombe and the Isle of Wight but they remain a fascinating puzzle.

From the 1820s we are on much firmer ground. What is certain is that William's first wife was Anne, maiden name unknown, and they, or at least she, had a daughter named Caroline who was baptised at St Andrew's, Clifton in Bristol on19 May 1822 followed by Amelia born on 20 April 1824 at 20 Richmond Place, Walcot, Bath and baptised at St Swithin's on 9 June. No record of their marriage has been found but it is thought that the couple lived in Mells from 1825-29. Nothing more is known about Anne except that she died at Mells on 30 October 1828 at the age of 40 and was buried on 3 November in St. Andrew's churchyard. The *Bath and Cheltenham Gazette* 30 October says that she was the wife of WW Wheatley the artist and lamented by all who knew her.[5] He is known to have been painting in Weston Super Mare in 1824 but nothing else is certain about that period.

Wheatley returned to Bristol soon after his wife's death and on the 24 June 1829, he married Emma Walker at St Paul's Church, Portland Square. Both were described as 'of this parish' meaning that they had lived there for at least three weeks during which time the banns would have been read. Emma was born in about 1809 the daughter of Thomas and Mary Walker a sawyer living in Road.[6] She was baptised at the parish church of Saint Lawrence on 24 December 1815 at the age of about five along with three of her siblings. William would have been 27 when they married just eight months after the death of his first wife Anne.

In a bizarre twist daughter Caroline was re-baptised at St Swithin's Walcot six months after the wedding on 27 December 1822 as 'Caroline Wheatley, base born, (illegitimate), daughter of Anne Wheatley of 15, Upper Camden Place, Bath'. What makes the situation complicated is that we don't know the date of William's marriage to Anne or the precise date of Caroline's birth but she would have been about seven years old and was still living with them in the 1841 census. She never married but had an illegitimate son named Thomas whose descendants moved to New Zealand, the forbears of John Friend. She was employed as a shoe binder who would have sewn together the upper leathers on a last. She died of peritonitis on 20 June 1850 at Bristol Infirmary, her age was given as 24 but according to her first baptism record she was 28.

A witness at Emma and William's wedding was James Baker Pyne (1800-1870) a self-taught landscape painter born in Bristol in 1800 who became a follower of Turner but at this time was one of the leading lights in what has become known as Bristol School of Artists which were mainly active in the 1820s. It was an informal association of both professional and amateur artists, sketching mainly landscapes in watercolours and oils, exactly the subjects and media that Wheatley was to make his own. His name does not appear

Sketching in Lullington Church c 1845

amongst their number but this is certainly where he learnt his craft. Pyne had some success as an artist and moved to London in 1835. Whether it was he that taught Wheatley the basics of landscape painting or the two of them learned together is not known but they must have been close for him to have been a witness at the wedding.

7

One of the patrons of the Bristol School was George Weare Braikenridge (1775-1856) born in Virginia but who lived most of his life in Bristol collecting antiques, paintings and ephemera. In the 1830s he commissioned Wheatley to provide extra illustrations for John Collinson's *History and Antiquities of the County of Somerset*, an edition which Braikenridge enlarged from two volumes to twelve. He was also commissioned to visit parishes to draw buildings of architectural or antiquarian interest. He was expected to choose suitable subjects and to gather ancillary information about the buildings and their contents, noting archaeological discoveries, alterations to buildings and demolition, and to gather information on local customs, genealogy, inscriptions on monuments and historical objects. The collection contains a few letters between the two men and is now held at the Museum of Somerset in Taunton.

William and Emma left Bristol and moved to her village of Road shortly after their wedding and son William Walter Wheatley II was born there in 1830 followed by Claude Lorraine Wheatley on 27 April 1834. Neither child was baptised at birth which means that we have not been able to trace the birthdate of William but that of Claude is known through an entry in a family bible.[7]

It is probable that he returned to Bristol in 1831 as he produced a number of depictions of the riots of that year. Two other members of the Bristol School also recorded the devastation, William James Muller and James Pyne - both his superior as artists. Nonetheless his reputation was well established in Frome as Thomas Bunn, a noted town philanthropist and solicitor recalls that in January 1837 on the coach to Bath he met two ladies from Road and,

> named to them an artist of the same village, who has attracted some notice at Frome. Mr Wheatley made a good drawing of Longleat House and Park which has been lithographed and sold in considerable numbers. This drawing and another of Nunney Castle have been copied on china at the manufactory. Others have appeared which are picturesque and in good taste. They did not appear to know that such a person existed.[8]

On another occasion in 1840 Bunn was present as Wheatley sketched a christening party of 200 near the church at Woodlands.

The census of 6 June 1841 for 1 Union Cottage Lane in Rode has: -
William Wheatley 36 artist
Emma Wheatley 31 wife
Caroline Wheatley 19 born outside the county
Claude Wheatley 8 scholar

Union Cottage Lane was the site of the poorhouse and is now part of Marsh Road. There were just the three people at home when the census was taken. Their eldest son, ten-year-old William Walter Wheatley II was not at there on the night, he was either down the road at a pub called the Three Horseshoes Inn or in a cottage next door, the record is not very clear, but he was staying with his maternal grandfather Thomas Walker a sawyer aged 69 and John Walker aged 19 also a sawyer. Amelia was 'living in' aged 17 as a servant to butcher Silas Dainton in Upper Street, a few streets from the family home. The Daintons were also members of the Road Baptist Church and in 1845 Silas took over as landlord of the Cross Keys eventually buying the freehold in 1852. Amelia is not mentioned in the census of 1851 so perhaps she left his employ before he moved to the pub. It is not clear today which cottage the family occupied but their house was described as still standing in 1918.[9]

Emma was baptised into the Road Baptist Church on 27 August 1843 at the age of about 32 along with nine others at an open-air baptism in the river at Road Bridge, the scene was painted by Wheatley and a copy now hangs in the church porch entitled simply 'The Baptising'. The Road congregation belonged to a branch of Baptist belief which followed the teachings of John Calvin and were known as Particular Baptists, a distinction far too complicated to go into here but their basic beliefs included adult baptism and the total immersion in water as shown in the painting. They were opposed to drinking, gambling, swearing, fornication outside of marriage and great emphasis was placed upon the individual's responsibility for their own salvation. The individual churches had a great deal of autonomy and were generally opposed to any form of state intervention in their practices.

In 1848 Shrove Tuesday fell on 7 March and Wheatley did one of his best-known paintings, capturing a ceremony known as the 'clipping' of St Lawrence church in Road. The word 'clypping' is Anglo-Saxon in origin, and derived from the word *clyp-pan*, meaning 'embrace' or 'clasp'. Little is known about its origins, though some think it was a Pagan custom with the purpose of creating a magical chain against the powers of evil. The villagers would hold hands, and form a circle around the church facing inwards and dance around the building. The dance ended with a huge shout which was supposed to drive away the devil for another year. Wheatley produced several versions of the event one of which is owned by Mr Alastair MacLeay and is reproduced here with his kind permission. The ceremony continues to the present day.

The Clipping of Road Church (Alastair MacLeay)

9

In July 1849 he wrote to Rev William Phelps the author of *The Antiquities of Somersetshire,* and as little is known about Wheatley's work and character it is worth copying it out in full,

I received yours of the 6th instant and was happy to hear from you. I envy you the pleasure you must have enjoyed in your continental tour, a happiness that I am fearful will not fall to my lot but since I saw you last, I have been sketching over three parts of the County of Somerset visiting *all* the churches & antiquities & I expect D.V. to visit the remainder. I am just returned from an unfortunate journey I have made in the neighbourhood of Porlock etc. having to travel to the various Parishes on foot with my bag and sketching implements, going over those *Hills* (Beautiful as they are) the Toil in travelling, the difficulties in finding the road etc I was overcome with fatigue, Taken ill, & was obliged to return home (having only finished six parishes after been out 8 or 9 days) just a day before I received your Note. I am now very unwell, but must endeavor to recruit Myself for another attempt. I am making these sketches for a private collection – independent of toil and Time the expense (economical as I am obliged to be) leaves me at the end of the sketching season poorer than when I started, there are a great many who pretend to be interested in these pursuits, but few really appreciate or understand them – I have no view by me of Farleigh House. The one I did for Col. Houlton is in the album in possession of one of the family. The Rev. E Jackson has I believe one or two views – I have not even a sketch. I think Mrs Jackson has that I saw on my way home through Bath at Everitts, Print Seller, Poultney Bridge, a Painting - a very good one – of the City of Bath. He told me it was painted for him & from which he is about to have a first rate Lithoprint, he has published several other views of Bath all very good, but the painting he showed me is the best view I have seen – but to Elaborate (sic) for a small view. Probably you might look at them – I was at Corsham some time back making a drawing for the Rev. Mr Jackson of the almshouse which is connected with the Hungerford History. I have not seen Mr Jackson for a long time. His church has I believe been restored, there was upon the old one a curious Sancte Cote[10] – I visited last summer Barton St. David, Somerset. I was agreeably surprised to find it more interesting than I expected – I wish with due Submission a little more elaborate description of the church had been given. It is rather a singular one from those around – I saw the Rev. Jn Ireland at his living of Queen Charlton. I was surprised to find in there but not after what I heard. He spoke to me about you & the work.

I Remain Dear Sir your Obt. St. W.W. Wheatley.

(P.S) have you seen the discoveries at Saint Cuthbert's, Wells? I have been there – they are really beautiful – I mean the Jesse & Lady Chapel. There was a brass inscription plate one of the Bishops found in the Cathedral.[11]

Rev Jackson was a well-known Wiltshire antiquary who was curate of Farleigh Hungerford from 1834 to 1845. His collection is now with the Society of Antiquaries in London and it is his account of Barton St David which Wheatley finds disappointing.

A cottage interior at Oare, Exmoor 1849 (Somerset Heritage Centre)

Wheatley's caption on the reverse of this touching scene reads: *Cottage Oare. The old woman after frying some bacon and eggs placed a wooden trencher on the table upon which she placed the hot frying pan and its contents from which the Driver & Guide helped themselves.* As at Lullington, he has included himself in the picture sketching the scene.

In January 1850 he was working for Rev. JHS Horner (1810-1874) of Mells Manor making a record of Somerset churches. It is estimated by John Friend that between 1,200 and 1,500 sketches were produced and that the Braikenridge Collection was completed by around 1851. In the census of 30 March 1851 Wheatley gives his age as 47 and his occupation as a 'landscape and antiquarian artist' living in Poor House Lane, Road with his wife Emma aged 42. The address is the same as Union Cottage Lane 10 years before but renamed, today it is known by its original name of Marsh Lane. The lane had been the home of the local workhouse until it was sold in 1838. Emma died at Road on the fourth of August1855 from a diseased heart which she had had for 'many years' and dropsy, or a swelling of the soft tissues due to a build up of fluid, described as a 'long and painful illness.'

On the 16 February 1854 Wheatley exhibited at the Society of Antiquaries in London, notice of which was published in *Proceedings of the Society,* vol.3 1856:-

Mr. W. W. WHEATLEY exhibited several Drawings in watercolour, executed by himself, of Churches and objects of Antiquity in Somersetshire and parts of Wiltshire; including the Fonts of the undermentioned Churches: 1. North Bradley, Wilts; 2. Melbury Bubb, Dorset; 3. Queen Camel, Somerset; 4. Broadway, Somerset; 5. Isle Abbot's, Somerset; 6. East Brent, Somerset; 7. Tickenham, Somerset.

11

By the summer of 1859 he had left the village and moved to Bath where on the 13th of July at the General Register Office he married his third wife Eliza Rogers daughter of William Rogers a brewer and his wife Sarah. Both gave their address as 3 Carriage Road, Widcombe not because they lived together but because it was cheaper to give one address than two. Eliza was 36 and William 57. The couple are joined by Eliza's mother Sarah now aged 73 and are living at 4 Carriage Road, William is now an, 'artist & landscape painter & of antiquarian subjects'. Next door at number 5 lived his eldest son William and wife Sarah whose lives are described below. They are still there at number 4 in 1864 when the road has been renamed Prior Park Road.

3-4 Carriage Road in 2021, now Prior Park Road

By the census of 1871 he and Eliza had moved to 8 Hatfield Buildings still in Widcombe and he was describing himself as a 63-year-old 'professor of landscape painting'. They took mother- in-law Sarah with them now aged 83 and blind.

In 1879 Wheatley exhibited at the Academy of Arts, 34 Milsom Street, Bath where he had three paintings on show 'Trowbridge, Wilts', 'Bradford Bridge and Chapel', and 'Near East Malling, Kent'. The pair continued to lodge in the Hatfield Buildings area with the 1884 Post Office Directory giving the address as 3 Woodbine Cottages, now demolished.

It is claimed that he became a recluse in old-age and largely estranged from his family. There are indications that he was reduced to hawking his sketches from town to town to earn a living. Perhaps his style of painting was no longer fashionable.

William died of 'paralysis' or what would now be called a stroke on the 1st of March 1885 at the age of 83 at 10 Waterloo Buildings, Bath, now demolished. Present at the death was Maria Maggs a 29-year-old charwoman who lived in the building with her husband Fred a valet. The 1881 census for that address includes four lodgers one of whom was a Mary Anne Wheatley aged 85 a widow receiving parish relief who was born in Bradford on Avon. She would have been born in around 1796 making her six years older than William and her history has

Hatfield Buildings Widcombe

been traced in part. In 1851 she was living at 3 Eldon Place, Walcot the widow of an army sergeant and aged 50. Ten years later she was a lodger at 9 Waterloo Buildings, and described as a pauper. It seems possible that she and William are related, probably by marriage and she may have been the reason for William's move to Bath after his wife died in 1855. Mary Wheatley died on 6 April 1885 aged 84 according to her death certificate and it is highly likely that he was visiting her at the time of his stroke and death. But who was Mary Anne? Presumably Wheatley was her married name and she was William's sister-in-law. Her husband has not been traced and had died so long ago that his first name had been forgotten by those who reported her death, all they knew was that he was a soldier named Wheatley, it seems possible that she was the wife of the yet to be found Ernest Wheatley and William's sister in law. She seems never to have worked and lived, 'off the parish' since at least 1850.

The other residents of Waterloo Buildings, the Maggs family, have a fascinating history of their own. Fred Maggs was the youngest son of the infamous William Maggs one of the leaders of a gang of career criminals from Frome. It was he and two others who were accused of the rape and murder of Sarah Watts in 1851 they were all acquitted and the crime remains unsolved. After William Maggs death the family moved from Frome to Bath and seem to have settled down to respectable occupations.

It seems that Wheatley was never far from poverty and that once one commission had ended he was pretty poor until he could find another. It has been mentioned that his paintings of the interior of churches are sometimes inaccurate and indeed one of his Frome paintings has moved the church tower to create a more pleasant composition and another has what looks like a Norman keep in the background. His draughtsmanship gives the appearance of being rather patchy; some are finally detailed and others very amateurish; his value lies in the recording of buildings and street scenes long since vanished.

There was an exhibition of his work in July 1911 held by the Somerset Archaeological and Natural History Society at the Mechanics Hall in Frome. Many of his paintings were lent by Mr ER Singer and Mrs W C Penny and some had been commissioned by Singer's father John Webb Singer, founder of the art metal company. He seems to have been largely forgotten in the early 20th

William Walter Wheatley 1802-1885 (Paula Antoniazzi)

century; there were questions asked in the pages of the journal, *Somerset and Dorset Notes and Queries* from 1917 about who the prolific artist who signed his work WWW could be.

Replies claimed that he was still well remembered by at least three residents of Rode where he was noted for his geniality and possession of a tame cuckoo.[12] It seems that he seldom, dated his work but the majority of those surviving seem to be credited to the 1840s and 50s.

As far as we know William had four children, two daughters with Anne and two sons with Emma. Little has been uncovered about the life of Amelia except for her time with Dainton the butcher and member of the Baptist church. It is believed that she never married but the others have been traced as follows: -

CAROLINE WHEATLEY 1822-1850

Caroline had an illegitimate son named Thomas whose descendant David Friend, Wheatley's great great grandson died in Waitakere Auckland, New Zealand in the 1990s. Caroline was six when her mother died and never married dying in 1850 at the age of 28. Thomas was brought up by William Walter Wheatley II and accepted as his son.

WILLIAM WALTER WHEATLEY II 1831-1868

Elder son William had found employment as a footman with the household of George Henry Bengough a magistrate and land owner and was living at his house, 20 Lansdown Crescent in Bath during the census night of 30 March1851. It is not known when his employment began but it did not continue for long after this. On 25 September 1852 records show that a WW Wheatley was baptised into the Road Baptist Church but it is not clear whether this was father or son. On the 25 December, William junior married Sarah Walker a native of Bristol at the Baptist, Pithay Chapel in that city. Footmen where expected to be young and unmarried and his employment would probably have been terminated at this time, something that he would have known before deciding upon marriage. The Baptist records for Road show that one of the William Wheatleys was paying pew money from December 1853 until June the following year. After the marriage the couple left Bath and returned to his village of Road where their daughter, Kate Caroline Emma Wheatley, was born during 1853 followed in 1855 by Ann Mary Wheatley. What he did for a living during this period is not known.

William was 'dismissed' to the Baptist Ebenezer Chapel at Widcombe, Bath on 23 June 1860. This is not as bad as it sounds, each chapel was autonomous and as William was leaving the area it was merely a recognition of that fact and acceptance that he will be joining another church (Road Baptist records). By the census of 1861 William II and the family were living at 5 Carriage Road Widcombe, Bath. Next door to his parents who were at number 4. He was now 31 years of age and employed as an attendant at the hot baths which does not sound as glamorous as a footman in the better part of Bath but at least he had some employment. Wife Sarah was working as a dressmaker but whether employed or on her own account is not stated. Their two daughters now aged seven and five were of course still at school.

Little is known about his life but in June 1867 a WW Wheatley applied to the City of Bath for the post of 'Inspector of Nuisances' a job not as amusing as it sounds as they were employed by the parish to inspect for offensive conditions (known as nuisances) that were in breach of the law, ie, bad sanitary conditions, smells, privies, gutters, refuse heaps etc. They also distributed disinfectant to ensure houses with small pox were protected. He was unsuccessful. According to David Friend the couple had four daughters none of whom married. William died in 1868 at the age of 39 and the family moved to London.

CLAUDE LORRAINE WHEATLEY 1834-1904

On the 6 April 1851 a few weeks before his 18th birthday son Claude was baptised into the Church of England at Tellisford with the ceremony performed by Charles William Baker the rector who was also Claude's employer. Claude worked at the mansion house, Baker's home, as a footman like his brother and it is quite likely that the baptism took place at his insistence as employing a 'heathen' in the house may not have been seemly.

Little more is known about Claude except that he became a butler having moved, by 1861, to 49 Seymour Street, Marylebone, London where he worked for George Ellison a solicitor at Lincolns Inn. Also working at the house was Maria Mead a housemaid aged 26 and on 1st October of that year they were married at Lexden in Essex. He left his once married to Maria and was reduced to what was possibly the lowest occupation in the land, an agricultural labourer, possibly their relationship caused a scandal resulting in the move to her hometown of Birch in Essex.

They had at least four children, daughters Rose 1863 and Emma 1866 followed by a son Claude in 1870 and Robert in 1895. They spent their married lives at Birch with Claude working as a domestic gardener until his death in 1904 at the age of 69. Maria lived on until May 1922 when she died at the age of 86. Claude has direct descendants now living in Ontario, Canada.[13]

Claude Lorraine Wheatley (Paula Antoniazzi)

Notes & Acknowledgements
In a future issue we hope to include more about Wheatley's work as an artist. The Adlam Collection is at the Society of Antiquaries in London and consists of a large collection of drawings inter- leaved with Collinson's History of Somerset. I have been greatly assisted in this research by Mr Peter Harris of Rode, Dr Phil Bendall of the Widcombe Association, Michael McGarvie FSA BEM of Frome and thanks are also due to Paula Antoniazzi a direct descendent of Claude Lorraine Wheatley now living in Canada for her permission to reproduce the photographs.

[1] Melcombe Regis baptisms from 1776
[2] David Friend to M McGarvie letter 19 November 1994
[3] Much information comes from a descendent of Thomas Wheatley, the natural son of Caroline one of Wheatley's daughters, David Friend in New Zealand who died in the 1990s. (Michael McGarvie)
[4] John Friend to M.McGarvie 1994-11-19
[5] I am again grateful to Michael McGarvie for this research.
[6] The original spelling of the village name was Rode but became corrupted to Road in the 1700s. The spelling used at the time is maintained throughout as it was not returned to its original form until 1919.
[7] I am grateful to Paula Antoniazzi great great great grandaughter of WWW now in Ontario Canada whose research posted on Ancestry has been invaluable.
[8] Derek Gill Bunn's Diary 'Experiences of a 19c Gentleman' FSLS p71
[9] Somerset and Dorset Notes and Queries vol 17 p.160
[10] A small gable or turret for hanging bells
[11] First quoted in Somerset and Dorset Notes and Queries vol.XXXII March 1987 By M. McGarvie the original is to be found in the British library Add.MS 33836 ff 258-59
[12] Somerset and Dorset Notes and Queries Vol 17 p.160
[13] Paula Antoniazzi personal communication.

FROME SOCIETY PUBLICATIONS ONLINE

Since its foundation in 1958 the society has produced around 100 books and pamphlets on the history of Frome and its surrounding villages. The majority of these have been out of print for many years and often the only surviving copy is to be found in the museum library. To avoid this research, being lost we are making copies free of charge in PDF format. This project will include some from other publishers. Hard copies are still to be found in the museum and the catalogue numbers are included below. The following titles are on the museum website (www.frome-heritage-museum.org) 'Search Our Collection' and more will follow.

The Poet of Beckington (Samuel Daniel 1562-1619)
Daphne Joy 1971 D10900

Westbarn Grange. The Story of a Farm, Witham Friary Parts 1 & 2 1600-1815
Michael McGarvie 1971 L582/3

Postlebury Hill, Cloford
Michael McGarvie 1971 L584

Nunney. An Historical Sketch
FSLS 1973 L634

A Light in Selwood A Short History of St. John's Church, Frome
Michael McGarvie 1976 L454

Nunney & Trudoxhill An Historical Sketch
Michael McGarvie 1977 L1848

Hardington Bampfylde Church
Michael McGarvie 1978 Redundant Churches Fund L692

The Sheppards & 18c Frome. A history of the important clothing family.
Derek Gill 1982 L855

The Antiquities of Mells, Elm & Buckland in 1730. John Strachey
Michael McGarvie 1983 L2457

Eleanor Vere Boyle Artist & Illustrator
Michael McGarvie 1983 L833

Orchardleigh House
Michael McGarvie 1983 L2441

The Making of Frome
Peter Belham 2nd edition 1985 L455

Sir Henry Newbolt & Orchardleigh
Michael McGarvie 1985 L912

Gardening at Marston House 1660-1905
Michael McGarvie 1987 L1297

St. Mary's Berkley
Michael McGarvie 1992 L1771

The Story of The Grange Tytherington
Michael McGarvie 1992 L1770

In the Steps of St. Hugh. 280 mile fund raising walk
Michael McGarvie 1994 Bush Publishing L3519

St. Mary Magdalene, Upton Noble
Michael McGarvie 1996 L3461

Orchardleigh Park & The Duckworths
Michael McGarvie. revised edition 1997 L2213

A VIEW OF KING STREET 1841

Antiquarius

King Street in the 1840s

This unusually detailed painting was produced in the 1840s by Walter William Wheatley whose life is outlined in the previous chapter. It captures a view taken from what is now Church Steps and its main focus is number17 the Three Swans Inn one of Frome's oldest pubs housed in a building dating from at least the 1600s or perhaps earlier. [1]

Wheatley's view from Church Steps in 2021

Frome architect and historian Rodney Goodall states of the inn that the 'central part is certainly a timber framed building, much disguised; the doorway, if not the door could be later 16th century but much added to and altered'. The earliest mention of the name comes from the churchwardens accounts in 1742 when the property was owned by Edward Whitchurch which isn't to say that the name was not in use long before. At the time of the painting the landlord was John Hamlett who reigned from around 1836 until 1847 and the front of the building is pretty much the same as it is today. Local historian Derek Gill states that 'the road improvements which followed the 1797 Turnpike Act resulted in a lowering of the street level outside the Three Swans so that two steps had to be added to all the buildings in the row. This may still be seen by looking at the front door and the base of the wooden jambs'.

The Three Swans in 2021

The property next door, proceeding downhill, number 16, **[2]** has a large pole sticking out of the door with a striped pattern suggesting a barber. It appears to be separate from the Three Swans and had, many years before, been occupied by James Vinney a shoe maker. There is what looks like a sign board above the left-hand window but it is not legible. Today the building retains much of its original shape but rebuilt, the doorway has gone and the ground floor windows have been replaced. A sketch of 1950 shows a doorway and shopfront to its left making the present arrangement of three lower sashes quite recent. The three upper windows are in about the same place but of recent date. When the two buildings were joined is uncertain but certainly by 1881 and unfortunately there are no occupiers listed in the 1841 census between the pub and the next business.

Next door, now number 15, the name BUNN can be seen above the doorway, **[3]** this was Henry Bunn, a brightsmith or worker in small objects made of white metal such as tin. He was in his mid 50s and lived there with his wife Martha. The property has had its gable replaced with a dormer window but retains the two windows on the first floor even though they are replacements. The door and shop front are in the same position with an enlarged shop window. From at least 1770 the building had been home to another pub the Nags Head but this seems to have closed by about 1800.

Proceeding further down the slope to number 14 **[4]** the property is described in the census as home to John Parker a labourer. It looks like another shop front but nothing further has been discovered about it and of course whoever ran the shop didn't necessarily live on the premises. the building was demolished after 1950.

In the distance framed by number 14 and the last building in Cheap Street is the once magnificent house known as Irongates, dating from the late 17th century but remodelled in about 1700. [5] In 1841 it was home to John Sheppard (1785-1879) a member of the family of clothiers and a founder member of the Frome Literary Institution to which he bequeathed his library. The books have long gone as have the magnificent grounds which once surrounded his house, now replaced by the drabbest of modern shopping centres. The property itself suffered the further indignity of having its beautiful stonework smothered in render and its interior used as a pet shop until recently. The property was in the occupation of the Sheppard family for 150 years until 1895.

Crossing the road and turning back up the hill we come to a building that is difficult to place in the census return [6] but formed the end of Cheap Street on the corner of King Street, possibly this was James Cox a draper and was until recently, Amica gifts and novelties.

The strange looking building on the corner of King Street and Eagle Lane, known as the 'Pepperpot' is now number 13 Cheap Street and has been described as the oldest building in Frome. [7] A former jettied building remodelled in the 18th century, there is not much left of it now apart from its footprint and its strange almost conical roof, its interior has been gutted and its exterior walls were replaced with plate glass before 1960. It stands at the extreme left of Wheatley's picture and the name HOLTON can just be made out in large letters below the first-floor windows. This was James Holton and family, a grocer. The property made the headlines in 1931 when some builders found part of a human jawbone and a hip bone walled up in an old window frame. Speculation was rife as to what had occurred, murder? buried

21

alive? Unlikely, the probable explanation is that the remains were washed out from nearby St. John's churchyard when its walls collapsed in 1799 and 'numbers of dead bodies rolled forth'. At the very bottom of Wheatley's picture can be seen two windows or possibly grills at ground level behind the flower sellers into which the bones might have rolled unnoticed. It is now La Strada coffee shop.

The 'Pepperpot' 13 Cheap Street in about 1902 and in 2021

Crossing the road once more we come to number 18 and again the name over the door can just about be made out as BUTLER [8], John Butler is recorded as a shoemaker aged 55 who lived there with his wife Elizabeth. She was still there as his widow in the 1851 census. He is seen leaning on bottom half of the stable door and there are what could be pairs of shoes hanging in his window. This tall building may be older than its fellows with what looks like a jettied front. The roughcast render has been in place for many years and may hide many clues to its age. It is now home to the Frome Bookshop.

The last building in King Street before it turns into Church Street [9] was that of James Edwards a painter and his family, now a fine corner building, number 19, it was probably two separate premises at this time and is now James Gaunt Interiors. All the old trades mentioned here had gone by the census of 1851.

BECKINGTON: A SELECTION OF GHOSTLY TALES

Dr David Davies

This small selection of ghost stories was collected by Dr David Davies, brother of the Reverend Bill Davies rector of Beckington in the 1980s and published as a small pamphlet by the Beckington Antiquarian Bookshop during that time.

Although, as is usual with such things, the tales are undated and unprovenanced they have a certain charm and are unlikely to have been recorded elsewhere. The author also included some tales from Wiltshire and even Sweden. I have picked out the local ones but left the remaining text as the original.

Original Cover illustration by John Dummett

ORCHARDLEIGH CHURCH

Orchardleigh church was supposed to be haunted by a bishop. The figure of a bishop is always seen pointing to part of the wall and when restorations are made in the 19th century, the body of a man was found under the wall with a pewter chalice at his side. This was the usual way to bury a bishop and the chalice is still kept in a safe place there being only four of these in England.

ORCHARDLEIGH LODGE

Some ghosts appear to prefer the daylight to make their appearance and others the night. One of these daylight hauntings is connected to one of the lodges. Close to one of them a man in dark clothes with a black beard will cross or glide in front of you with a very long curved knife in his hand, and look at you the whole time while he is crossing. He makes no acknowledgement to your hale, just a fixed stare that you get in return. Once over the road he disappears into the building. He is of rough appearance and scowling. Why he should walk across with a knife in his hand is strange, for at that actual place there is no particular path.

LULLINGTON CHURCH

This is another daylight appearance, seen by several people for about five minutes, but not actually in the church, usually when one is leaving the church. Almost accompanying you, will be seen a tall figure all dressed in black, right down to his feet, on his head he has a tall hat with a narrow brim – very much like a Welsh hat. In fact, typical puritan dress. He accompanies you to the church gate and there he leaves you and even though you look up and down the road you see no one. Also, just opposite the church is the school house, but it may have been the vicarage at one time. This is also haunted by a similar figure. It is only afterwards that we realise that we really saw a ghost. At other times a hooded figure is quite often seen in the region of Lullington but usually late at night.

LULLINGTON GREEN

Lullington is also the only village recorded that has a haunted green. On those English summer nights when everything is stilled a constant whispering is heard as if persons are planning a conspiracy. Occasionally a loud abrasive voice will be heard above that of his fellows, then it will subside once more into mutters followed by further raucous voices. One can sense them crouching around some ancient fire, a stance that wild men will adopt when the embers and long shadows are before them. Strange to say not a word can be heard clearly. The trial of some of Monmouth's men was probably held in the village, there were certainly courts held in the village - Lullington has not always been so peaceful.

THE LEGIONNAIRE

In Lullington there is actually a Roman bridge, what other village in England could boast of one! It has a Roman inscription upon it. However, no legion of Romans go marching over it as on the Roman roads as on the Downs near Devizes, presumably going to their deaths in an ambush by the ancient Britons. But this bridge is simply haunted by one solitary soldier who like brave Horatius seems intent upon keeping the bridge at all costs. He can be seen there sometimes late at night in full dress with spear glistening in the moonlight.

Ye olde Houses, Beckington.

A village view from around 1905

BECKINGTON VILLAGE.

One of the oldest houses in the village of Beckington has a very wide staircase which is supposed to be haunted. Several of the people who have lived there for a length of time have told me about it, in fact, now that they have left they feel rather lonely without it. The house is right on the main road. During the late-night hours, when the noise of the traffic is still the ghosts stir. Upon the stair is heard a rustling and creaking accompanied by movement and whisperings. There was every impression that the stairway was very busy with persons in elaborate clothes. If it had occurred only occasionally they would have thought it strange but as it is nearly every night they got quite used to it. There was also some space that they could not account for in the centre of the old house. They had the feeling that there was at one time a spiral staircase there but they never got down to investigate it thoroughly.

After they had been at the house for several years they rearranged some of the furniture. They placed an old Welsh dresser against some panelling in one of the rooms and it immediately began to give out too many creaks to be natural; they put it down to the road. In the early morning when the husband went down to get his wife a cup of tea, one plate from the dresser lay in his path on the stairs and as he went by on his way back up the dresser was swaying as if in an earthquake and one more plate rolled off to shatter. When they got up they cleared up the mess. The next day it was the wife's turn to make the tea and bring it up and nearly all the plates began to roll about and more fell off and smashed. For the sake of saving the remaining plates and jugs, they moved the dresser only a few feet to the side and there was no more trouble. They took some of the panels out and found to their surprise indications of an ancient spiral staircase. What they had done, it was suggested, was to place the dresser right in front of the head of the stairs which had discomfited the ghost of the house. They found afterwards that if they put anything light like a chair in the same place where they had the dresser, it was

25

sure to be turned over in the morning. They wanted to make sure that the present occupiers knew who the house belongs to!

MILL LANE, BECKINGTON

There is a real little old country lane that leads off the main road, well-liked by countrymen loving a Sunday evening walk after church, the trouble is that it is rather short. As its name signifies, it leads to a mill – a watermill. After descending the hill there is a quaint a little cottage on the left that overlooks the river Frome, it is the most delightful spot that one could imagine. A few years back it was inhabited by an old lady, Mrs Wise, full of folklore who had a dog and several wise looking cats. She would always offer you a glass of home-made wine; she had been a milliner at one time. One day when I went to visit her she was shaking like a leaf and told me that she had been kept awake all night by screaming coming from the direction of the mill. She said that she was too scared to go out and I was the first person to see her that day. The dog also looked scared. In fact, the cries were often heard in the dead of night and a very strange thing is that no dog likes to pass up that road even in daylight. A clairvoyant who lives in the village has visited the spot and said that there is definitely the body of a woman somewhere at the side of the road. In olden times when the trees were allowed to grow, it must have been a very lonely and eerie spot indeed.

BERKELEY LANE

Just leading out of Beckington, beyond the castle, is a little lane which goes past what I always think, especially on the winters night, is a gruesome cemetery that once belonged to the chapel. This lane is haunted, not in the night but in the twilight. If you follow this lane down it will lead you eventually to St George's Cross. When you get into the hollow at the bottom equidistant between the cemetery and the crossroads, if it is still a winters evening just look back along the way you have come and you will hear a shushing noise and a clippity clop - the feet of a horse touching the road after it has come over the hedge and then there is no more. You won't hear it again that evening but repeat the process on the following night and there it is again.

A VICAR OF MELLS

Only a few miles away as the crow flies is the village of Mells which boasts a very lovely church and statues but it is well haunted. When a church is haunted it is usually extremely so. Generally, ghosts do not make themselves apparent in the daytime but in this church as we go in and start to roam around we are not usually alone there is the cleaner, the sexton or even the vicar hovering around. We can be dimly aware of a tall figure in a cassock who seems to be active in the chancel and we each go about our little businesses. Suddenly, however he glides over to us and seems to take a great interest in us, in fact too close for comfort, his eyes seem blazing or simply angry. We prepare to depart but he seems to pass right through us and we get a strange and horrible feeling that it is no longer 'I' but 'We'. This lasts for a few hours after the encounter and the feeling wears off - or does the 'It' gradually leave us and go back to where we first picked him up?

WILLIAM SMITH'S GEOLOGICAL MAP OF SOMERSET

Peter Wigley

William Smith (1769–1839), surveyor and geologist, was born on 23 March 1769 at The Forge, Churchill, Oxfordshire, the son of John Smith (1735–1777), the village blacksmith, and his wife, Ann (1745–1807). He was educated at the village school, which he attended until about 1780. In 1787 Smith became assistant to the land surveyor Edward Webb (1751–1828) at Stow on the Wold, learning to measure and value land. Webb, according to Smith, was 'possessed of great ingenuity and skill in mechanics, mensuration, logarithms, algebra and fluxions' and evidently taught Smith well. In 1791 the young 22-year-old William Smith was asked by Webb to survey an estate near High Littleton in Somerset belonging to Lady Elizabeth Jones. He made the journey on foot from his employer's house in Stow-on-the-Wold down to Stowey in Somerset, a distance of over 80 miles.

As part of this survey, Smith was required to go underground at the Mearns Colliery in High Littleton and it was here that he first became acquainted with geology. The geology of the Somerset coalfield is much more complicated than in many other parts of Britain; the coal seams are often steeply inclined and are frequently faulted. Smith's introduction to geology would have been aided by the practical knowledge of the miners. Smith also had in his possession a cross-section across the coalfield which had been made more than 70 years previously by the talented John Strachey[1]. During the course of the survey Smith began to understand the sequence of the strata which he encountered. In addition to the various seams of coal, he recognized sandstone, locally known as greys, shales (clift) and fireclay (pan). Surveying in these dark, wet and cramped condition must have been no easy job, especially as Smith was not a small man.

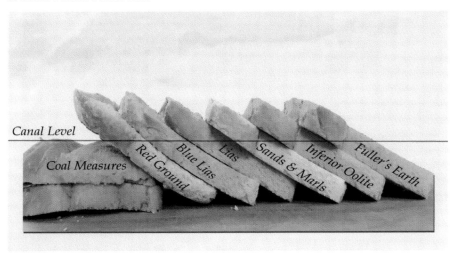

Smith's 'Slices of Bread analogy describing the succession of strata in the Somerset Coal Canal

Coal had been mined in Somerset for many centuries but poor roads made it difficult to transport. In late 1792 there was a proposal to build a canal in order to carry coal across the country via a new developing canal network. Smith's work on the High Littleton survey evidently impressed Lady Jones and other nearby landowners, including Jacob Mogg, Samborne Palmer and James Stephens, who were all to become shareholders in the canal, for in due course he was to become the canal surveyor. Part of Smith's task was to survey a route for the canal which maintained, as much as possible, a constant elevation (level) in both branches of the canal. Smith, always the astute observer, saw that along the level, strata were gently inclined to the east or southeast and used the analogy of superimposed slices of bread and butter to describe what he saw.

His nephew wrote in his *Memoirs of William Smith* that 'in each of the levelled lines the strata of 'red ground', 'lias' and 'freestone' came down in an eastern direction and sunk below the level, and yielded place to the next in succession' These observations became fundamental to Smith's concept of the strata and their order, as was his use of the fossils contained within them. Smith was an avid collector of fossils, not for their curiosity value but as tools which helped to define the various strata. In a thoughtful memorandum written in the Swan Inn at Dunkerton he remarked on the 'wonderful order and regularity with which Nature has disposed of these singular productions (fossils), and assigned to each class its peculiar stratum'. Eventually, in 1799, Smith produced his first Table of Strata.

It seems likely that Smith may have been inspired to make his first geological map after seeing a coloured soil map around Bath published by Billingsley and Davis in the 1798 edition of the Somerset County Agricultural Report. Using a copy of Taylor and Meyler's *Map of Five Miles around the City of Bath*, Smith coloured the geological distribution of the Oolite, Lias and Triassic 'Red Ground'. This map is arguably one of the first geological maps ever made.

Facsimile version of the Taylor and Meyler map of Five Miles around the City of Bath, geologically coloured bv William Smith in 1799

28

Smith later made another more detailed version of the geology around Bath and went on to colour the county geologically on a one inch to one mile copy of the Day and Masters (1782) map of Somerset. In 1805, at an agricultural gathering in Woburn, he showed the map to the Duke of Clarence (later William IV). Smith wrote to a friend telling him 'happened to have my large map of Somersetshire with me, which I have lately completed, as a specimen of what may be done upon all the county maps in the kingdom.' Unfortunately, this map was subsequently lost and was not included in the atlas of county geological maps which Smith later completed. In 1815 John Cary published Smith's pioneering map *A delineation of the strata of England and Wales, with part of Scotland* which covered Somerset but not in the detail with which Smith originally mapped it.

Smith's famous 1815 map, A Delineation of the Strata of England and Wales, with part of Scotland

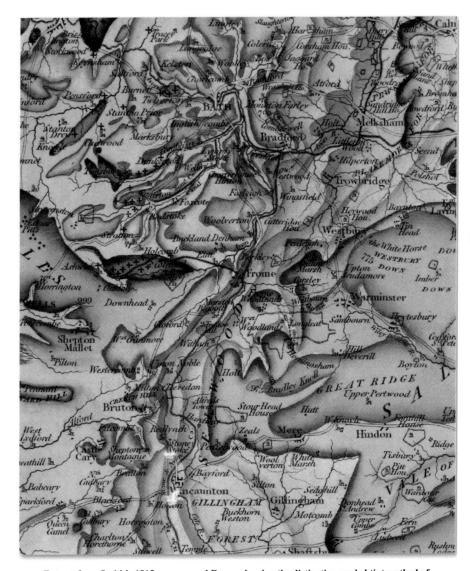

Extract from Smith's 1815 map around Frome showing the distinctive graded tint method of geological colouring used by Smith. The technique gives an almost three-dimensional effect to the map.

This may have been the end of the story but for what appears to have been a slipshod, but fortuitous, mistake made on the part of John Cary's sons, George and John. They published a topographic map of Somerset inadvertently using an early copper plate upon which Smith's geological line work of the county had been engraved. The geological lines suggest that this was a preliminary version, albeit incomplete, of Smith's long-lost map. With the aid of modern image processing, all pre-existing hand-colouring of the hundreds, roads and other boundaries on the original map were removed and the de-coloured version loaded into a Geographic Information System (GIS). Once in the GIS, the map was spatially adjusted to fit both with Smith's 1815 map and modern geological data sources. The original line work was geologically interpreted in order to re-create, as far as possible, Smith's original map. It was most important to honour all of Smith's geological lines but, at the same time, not to over-interpret them based on modern knowledge

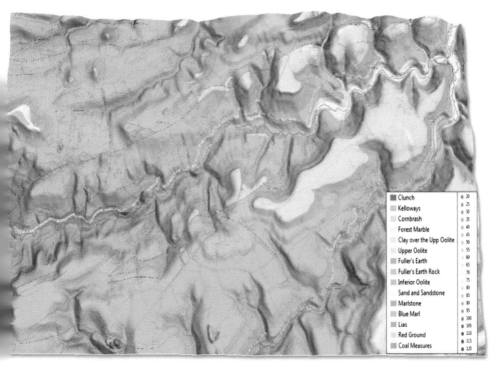

Modern geology of the Somerset Coal Canal area expressed using Smith's names for the strata. The Coal Measures are to the right of the map, the northern branch of the canal traverses the Red Ground (Triassic), Lias, Inferior Oolite and Fuller's Earth. The constant level of both branches of the canal is shown by modern Lidar elevation data (metres)

In addition to his accomplishments as a geologist and mapmaker, Smith drained land and created water meadows, advised on sea defences and, importantly, was concerned with the exploration for coal and other minerals. Coal powered the industrial revolution and was a much sought-after commodity, particularly among wealthy landowners. Smith was involved in numerous trials for coal, several of which were in Somerset. One of these trials was in 1804 at Batheaston near Bath. Smith correctly predicted that Red Ground (Triassic) would occur below the Lias (Jurassic) and assumed that productive Coal Measures would occur below. Shafts were sunk at Batheaston but unluckily Coal Measures were absent. Instead they encountered a sandstone, now known as Chromhall Sandstone, part of the Carboniferous Limestone sequence, below the Coal Measures. An unwelcome side effect of this coal trial may have been the disruption to water supply in the nearby Bath Thermal Springs. Smith opened up the hot springs and restored supplies which serendipitously coincided with his successful efforts to stem water flowing into the mine.

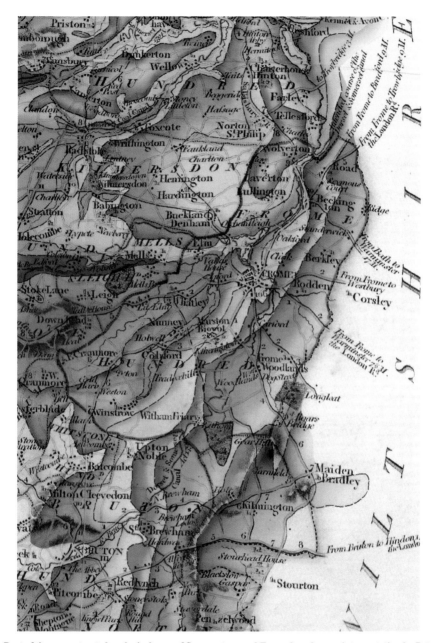

Part of the reconstructed geological map of Somerset around Frome based on an interpretation by Peter Wigley of Smith's geological lines engraved on the 1829 Cary map

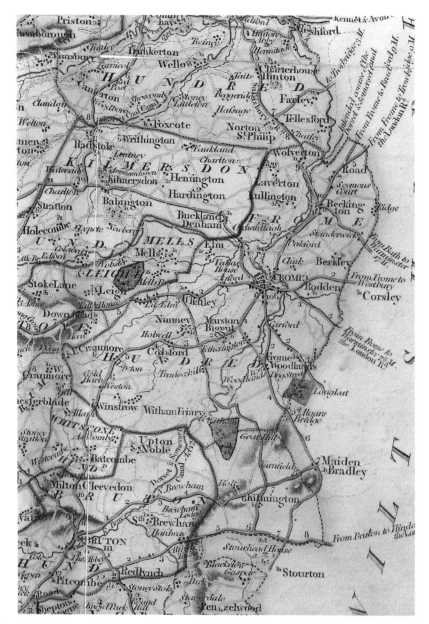

Part of a *New Map of the County of Somerset* published by G. & J. Cary in 1829 around Frome used for the reconstruction of the geology of Somerset. The map clearly shows Smith's engraved geological lines; there are no legend tablets and no other mention of the lines is made (from the collection of Hugh Torrens).

In 1805, Smith visited the site of another intended colliery at Cooks Farm at South Brewham, to the south of Frome. His examination of spoil from the bottom of the pit revealed a particular fossil which Smith knew to be characteristic of the Kelloways Stone at the base of his Clunch (Oxford) Clay. From this Smith immediately knew that the trial was far too high in the geological succession for coal to be encountered. John Phillips wrote in *Memoirs of William Smith* that 'in spite of remonstrances from Mr Smith and his intelligent

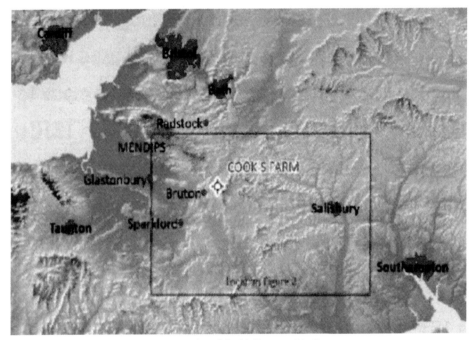

The location of Cook's Farm coal trail

friends, the speculators proceeded at a ruinous expense'. Operations continued until 1807 when, at a depth over 600 feet, the shaft became flooded. This effectively ended mining operations and bankrupted several speculators.

William Smith died on the 28 August 1839; he rose from humble beginnings and for much of his life he received little or no encouragement from the gentlemen-scientists of the geological establishment. His work was often plagiarized and he endured a period of imprisonment for debt. Yet for all this, during his lifetime, he accomplished great things. He made the first geological map of England and Wales and pioneered the science of stratigraphy. His great achievements were eventually recognized and he was later acknowledged as one of the pre-eminent scientists of his generation.

[1] Michael McGarvie, John Strachey FRS and local Antiquaries in 1730, Frome Society Yearbook 13, 2009

More details of William Smith's work are available at the website www.strata-smith.com
Ed

COCKEY'S MANOR II

Since the last issue two more photographs of the demolition of the old mansion in Spring Road have emerged courtesy of Steve Horler and taken by Fleming Krage in 1972

FRAUD, MANSLAUGHTER & TRANSPORTATION

The Candy family of Marston Bigot 1839

Mick Davis

The Candy family were yeoman farmers living and farming at Marston Bigot headed by their mother Hannah described as a good-looking woman in her 40s with a tolerable education who had been left the huge sum of £7,000 by her father and who had been separated from her husband for the past four years. On 22 January 1839 her eldest son Thomas went to a solicitor, a Mr Whittington in Bath, wanting to mortgage some land; he said that his father had just died and that he and the family wished to raise some money. Mr Whittington came out to the farm a week later, viewed the land and collected some deeds from the Candy family, which consisted at the time of Hannah, the mother, Thomas, the eldest son and other sons Francis, Theophilus, and William. The deeds were impressive documents one, dating from 1810, was a lease signed by the Marquis of Bath and others were signed by the Earl of Cork & Orrery. Everything requested by Whittington was produced and seemed to be in good order and the mortgage amount of £490 was handed over to the Candy family by Frome grocer and money lender Edward Gibbons.

Then the plan started to go wrong. It seems that Thomas got greedy and went back to Whittington asking to borrow further monies against a field named Railmead that he claimed an uncle named Selby had given him, again he produced deeds and paperwork to back this up. Whittington thought that he had better see the land himself to make sure that all was in order. He rode over to the field and met a Mr Butt who was in charge of collecting local land taxes. In the course of making his enquiries he was astonished to learn not only that no one by the name of Selby had lived or owned land in the area but that Thomas Candy's father, also Thomas, was very much alive and well, and having split from his wife was living in Cloford about five miles away with his sister!

The outcome of these revelations was that on 22 November, officers raided their farmhouse, and the five family members were arrested, taken to Bath and charged with forgery. According to reports this took place with the active assistance of the estranged husband. After the magistrates became satisfied that there was a good case against them, and with forged documents 'covering the magistrates table' they were remanded to Shepton Mallet jail.

The Candy family along with James Sealy stood trial on 2 April 1840 at the Taunton Assizes. The Earl of Cork & Orrery gave evidence in person to say that the documents in his name were forgeries. Edward Brimson landlord of the George in Frome was called and stated that he had worked for the Marquis of Bath for 19 years until his death and was certain that the various documents contained forgeries of his lordship's signature. The court was told that the deeds had been executed by a master hand and bore every resemblance to old deeds, the parchment had been discoloured, the wax looked as though it had faded from age, the tape had completely lost its colour and some very old stamps had been affixed to the parchment. The engrossing, or final copy of the documents was also in a very old-fashioned style, 'a better deception was perhaps never practised' and executed with such skill that they 'could have deceived the Lord Chancellor himself'.

When asked to account for his actions Thomas Candy came up with the following:

> I met a person from Frome of the name of Sealy who was a clerk to different attorneys; I told him I wanted to borrow some money on some papers I had at Marston. He obtained the papers from me and when he returned them he told me I could procure the money at Bath. I took them to Mr Whittington who came and saw the property. Mr Whittington left £50 at our house and said he wanted one or two more papers. I told Sealy of this and he desired me not to trouble myself about it and he would get them for me. He afterwards brought them and I took them to Mr Whittington's office.... he informed me that there must be a declaration. This I gave to Sealy who said he would take it to Lord Cork and get his signature. Sealy told me to inform Mr Whittington that my father was dead and I said that he was dead in the eyes of the law in consequence of his bankruptcy. I gave Sealy about £10 pounds at different times for his trouble. After the transaction of £490 was over I went again to Mr Whittington and requested him to advance me £100. He said he would on my producing security. This I told Sealy, who said he would make me something on which I could obtain the money. He did so and I took the papers to Mr Whittington who advanced me £15 on account. Seeley told me everything was alright, and I thought it was so. He is about 50 years old and blind of one eye.

All the defendants claimed that they signed the documents without realising what they were. The youngest son, Ferdinand who would have been about 18 at the time was not involved in the trial but when shown the documents he declared them to be in Sealy's handwriting.

Thomas was convicted of 'Feloniously uttering certain forged & counterfeit deeds' and being the instigator of the scheme, he was sentenced to be transported for 15 years. From his prison description book we know that he was 5 feet 8 inches tall, of slight build, hazel eyes, married and could read and write well. He was moved to the prison hulk *Stirling Castle* at Devonport on 7 May 1840 and on the 25 August put aboard ship, the *Lord Lyndoch* for the journey to Australia. On 4 October he was examined by the ship's doctor who described him as, 'A man of robust form but of irritable temperament and suffering much from mental instability, was admitted to hospital complaining of headaches, extreme languor, depression of spirits and general pains. Appears weighed down by grief and despair. Head painful, ideas confused.' The doctor's diagnosis was that he is suffering from a fever, rheumatism of the right hip and thigh, 'so much so as to confine him to bed' and dysentery. He has become delirious and 'seldom speaks to anyone unless spoken to and then answers in unconnected sentences', by 9 November, 'his mind appears entirely gone, he lays on his back with constant nervous twitching, countenance cadaverous, constantly muttering until death claimed him on the 11th.'

Mother Hannah, aged 50 and son William were convicted of the lesser offence of conspiracy to defraud and were sentenced to two years each; Francis & Theophilus were acquitted of uttering forged deeds. Hannah was granted a free pardon and discharged on 2 May1841 and was back at her farm by the census of 6 June aged 50 with sons Theophilus 24, Ferdinand 20 and daughter Hannah aged 14.

The undoubted star of this whole sorry affair was James Sealy. He managed to avoid the general roundup of the Candys and the magistrate's initial investigations but was 'betrayed by a Judas friend' under the false impression that there was a £50 reward for his capture. Once apprehended he was brought to Bath on 2 December in the custody of Mr Ivey one of the Frome constables. It seems that he had been living in Coleford with his wife Mariah who was still there in the census of 1841 aged 48 but no further details are known. Contemporary reports take up the story:

He is 42 years of age but it appears considerably older and he has lost the sight of his right eye. He is of very diminutive size and was shabbily dressed. He was very facetious and related many anecdotes of his chequered life, coolly observing that he supposed that he had obtained some notoriety in the world and that his name it would be handed down to posterity. He requested as a favour that he might be allowed sight of the *Police Gazette* in which he was advertised as having been excluded from Frome…. He read the description with great glee and observed that the officers do not understand the business and were only bunglers, "For (said a prisoner laughing immoderately), instead of being blind in my left eye it happens to be my right one! Pshaw! What a libel to say I turn in my toes, (the *Hue and Cry* so describes his walk) as to the black glazed hat, that I consigned to the tomb of the Capulets, well knowing it would be a conspicuous mark, and the light trousers I exchanged for black ones. When he came to that part which describes him as a clever writer, Aye (explained at the prisoner evidently much flattered), they have hit it for there is not a man born whose handwriting I cannot imitate". But yet he was highly indignant when he read that his wife was supposed to be hawking tape around the country. No, (said the prisoner with emphasis) she does not sell tape, but manufactures lace of the finest quality and is an excellent judge of the article.

The prisoner then proceeded to say that he had filled the several offices of Vestry and magistrates clerk and many other responsible situations. "But, (remarked he) there are many vicissitudes in the game of life and I'm here now a prisoner fully resigned to my fate which will be transportation for life. At any rate they cannot say that I have not learned philosophy".

Throughout the entire interview Sealy remained perfectly calm and composed; he asked for pen and paper before proceeding to write out his confession which was basically in line with the prosecution case, stating that Thomas Candy had approached him having heard that he was a master at producing documents. He went to visit the family and found Mrs Candy dressed in mourning and Thomas with crape around his hat explaining that his father had just died. Sealy produced the required deeds for the family and delivered them. He made the ink by mixing it with some garden mould and tinged the red ink with a little black, the tape he discoloured with vinegar. Thomas thought them too clean and proceeded to rub them a little with coal ash. The conspiracy proceeded well until Thomas let slip in conversation that his father was still alive; Sealy declared that had he known this he would not have written a single word and that the affair was now sure to be discovered and that they should all be hanged.

In front of the Bath magistrates sitting in Chandos House on 19 December Sealy was shown the forged documents and examined them with the greatest deliberation and with the air of a complete man of business. A slight smile passed over his countenance as he proudly inspected the signatures, tape and wax on the pile of parchment in front of him before announcing to the court that, "They are all my handwriting." Having commented upon the charges his statement took a different turn and he talked at length about the Candy family which was commented upon in the local newspaper:

'We refrain from giving the latter part of the prisoners statement, hoping for the credit of human nature it is not true, as it relates to alleged most horrid and dreadful threats uttered by that part of the family who are now in custody against the father. A thrill of horror pervaded the whole court on hearing the alleged imaginations of the son against the parent.'

Sealy blamed drinking for his life's misfortunes and said that he intended to plead guilty; Colonel Baily, the magistrate, sent him off to Ilchester jail. He gave thanks that he was not committed to Shepton as that was where the Candys were confined. Little has been discovered about the details of his life but he was the son of an ironmonger named John and came originally from 'a good family' in Tetbury in Gloucestershire, one of seven brothers most, if not all, in respectable occupations concerning the metal working trades. He had married twice, firstly, Anna Tomlins a widow of Sutton Benger in Wiltshire in March 1820 and settled down to life as a shopkeeper in that village. He arrived in Frome about three years before his arrest and on 14 September 1835 he married his second wife Maria Rayne at St John's in Frome and by the time of his arrest he had fathered three children by his two wives including a son named Lorenzo in 1821. He had been working as a clerk for Mr Thomas T Hawkes, a solicitor with offices in North Parade, Frome. At his trial the charges were read out as follows;

> Feloniously forging certain deeds purporting to have been signed and sealed by the Right Honourable Edmund Earl of Cork and Orrery whereby Thomas Whittington was defrauded of a large sum of money, also with having, cut, torn and got off the impressions of stamps donating duties under the care and management of the commissioners of stamps from certain parchments with intent to use the same upon other parchments chargeable with the said duties. Also with having feloniously & fraudulently used joined and affixed upon certain parchment stamps which had been cut off from other parchments.

In reply to the charges he stated that,

"I am afraid sir that my life has been wild and irregular, but it is now too late to retrieve it." and quoted his motto as "Dum Vivimus vivamus" (While we live let us enjoy life.)

As expected on the 2 April 1840 at the County Assizes in Taunton before Justice Coltman, James Sealy was sentenced to transportation for life.

Despite his courtroom bravado Sealy must have decided, upon reflection, that a convict life was not for him and on 4 May he petitioned the Marquis of Normandy, then Home Secretary in the hope of receiving a pardon. He stated that upon his apprehension he had made a full confession to the offence which he claimed it was instigated by others for their own advantage and now expressed the greatest contrition for his conduct and asked for the case to be mitigated in whichever manner his Lordship saw fit. The document was signed by 49 people from his home town of Tetbury but was to no avail. Worse was to come. His relief at not being confined in the same space as the Candy family was short lived as on the 7 May they were lumped together with others and sent aboard the prison hulk *Stirling Castle* moored at Plymouth. Whether they met on board is not recorded but Candy may well have made it his business to seek out Sealy, once fellow conspirator but now arch enemy, and on 7 September 1840 they sailed on the *Lord Lyndoch* to exile Tasmania.

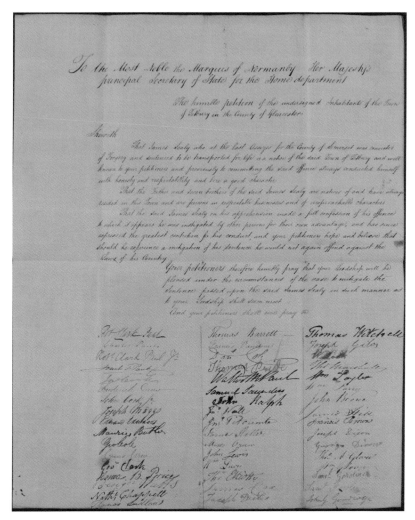

Petition to the Marquis of Normandy May 1840

The *Lyndoch's* description book described Sealy as aged 43, 5 feet 3 inches tall with a dark complexion black hair and grey whiskers. As noted before he was blind in his right eye but something else was added, which had not been mentioned before, his right hand was described as 'crippled'. When and how did this happen? Did Candy catch up with him in prison or aboard the prison hulk and exact a fitting revenge on the man he saw as the author of his woes by removing the possibility of his ever returning to his trade of scrivener or clerk? As a skilled draughtsman with a talent for advancing himself Sealy would have made himself very useful to the authorities and businesses that ran Tasmania but at 43 with one eye and presumably unable to write he would have been no use to anyone and his future very bleak.

Prison hulk Stirling Castle at Plymouth

On 1 January 1841 Sealy reported to the sick bay with 'icterus' or jaundice and was discharged a week later on 8 January. There is no mention of any injury to him received during the voyage and his name does not appear in the section of the surgeon's report book reserved for injuries sustained onboard.

The ship arrived on 5 February 1841 and having survived the rotting hulk of the *Stirling Castle* and the hazardous voyage to the other side of the world on the *Lord Lyndoch* he died at New Town Bay, Hobart on 28 February 1841 at the age of 43.

*The Candy family had suffered tragic circumstances five years before as detailed in the book, *Foul Deeds & Suspicious Deaths in and around Frome* by Mick Davis & David Lassman.

The Lord Lyndoch's record of Sealy's death

A HOUSE ON PORTWAY STEPS.

Dr John Harvey 1977

The house now numbered 32 Christchurch Street East, formerly 26a, consists of two main parts of different dates. A cottage probably dating from the early 18th century runs north-south along the west side of Portway Steps. At right angles is a more modern block fronting the street. Its high-pitched eastern gable rises above the southern end of the cottage at the corner of the steps; at the west it butts upon the next house, number 30. Both parts are of traditional masonry and of two storeys. The front slope of the roof is of plain clay tiles, the other roofs are of pantiles. There are no inscriptions or dates anywhere on the building.

The title deeds proved disappointing as they reached only to 1900, but the abstract mentioned the lease of 1885 granted by the Marquis of Bath. This showed that the property had belonged to the Longleat Estate which sold the freehold in 1927. The lease granted on 31 March 1885 was for 99 years to John Vallis, a Frome carpenter and builder of the whole block between Christchurch Street and Vicarage Street, and stretching from Plumbers Barton on the west to Portway steps. Mr Vallis who became a builders merchant in a large way, went bankrupt in 1900 and his leasehold was sold at auction on 31st October. The purchaser was Frederick Snook a general dealer who died on 26 March 1919 leaving the premises to his wife Harriet Snook who sold on 10 October 1921 to Mr Percy Robert Oswick a piano tuner already in occupation as her tenant. Mr Oswick died on 1 January 1962 and on 17 August his widow Annie Caroline Oswick conveyed the property to Walter Challice who sold it to my wife and myself on 30 September 1975.

32 Christchurch East in 2012

The cottage along Portway Steps corresponds with a building shown on the earliest detailed map of 1744. On the other hand, the front block of the street had not been built when another map was surveyed in 1870, though the adjacent house, number 30 (formally 26) appears on the Cruse map of 1813. The cottage and the front block are linked by a handsome staircase in a spacious hall. The stairs seem to be of mid 18th century date, but may have been brought from some other house. Later than the front block is the kitchen with the bedroom above it facing north into the garden. These were built of brick and the roof rests on the top rafters of the front block having a flatter slope. At the internal angle another addition was built, comprising a lobby and pantry beneath and a bathroom above in a mixture of brick and stone. This work was probably of the 1880s to judge from a Gothic window in the bathroom.

The staircase at 32 Christchurch Street East in 2000

Most of the earlier history house comes from the Longleat estate documents deposited in the Wiltshire Record Office, now in Chippenham. This was pointed out to me by Michael McGarvie, who most generously provided early references to the area. The first mention is a lease (Survey Book 845/3,222) from Lord Weymouth, (Sir Thomas Thynne 1640-1714, first Viscount Weymouth), to John King a wiredrawer on 17 July 1696. This was for 99 years or the lives of King, his wife Hester, and their son Joseph, of the whole block except for the northern corner to Vicarage Street at the foot of Plumber's Barton. The site was then known as, 'Up in Town' a name used for the slope between Vicarage Street and the old road, 'Behind Town', now known as Christchurch Street East. In 1712 (845/3,185) the northern corner, a house which was formally a barn with 40 feet of garden, was leased to James West a clothier. It had formally been held by a James West, now deceased and was on the lease for the lives of the younger West, his uncle Stephen Kipping and his nephew Thomas Andrews.

By 29 September 1747 both leases had fallen in, and the whole block was granted to Thomas Lacy a carpenter, (845/3,178) for his life, (he was then 46 and died on 9 September 1762), and those of his wife Elizabeth, who died 14 May 1792 and their daughter Ann then aged six, (still living in 1812). Meanwhile, the Manor of West Woodlands to which this area belongs had been surveyed in 1744 by John Ladd who made a large map, (D14) as well as a detailed book, (845vol.10) the map shows the main part as Sc.1 and West's smaller piece on Vicarage

Street as Hf.1. The only building shown on the main block corresponds with the cottage wing of number 32 along the southern part of the west side of the street lane which became Portway Steps.

The survey book describes plot Sc.1 as 'late Kings. Ye House down'.

A condition of the lease of 1747 was that Lacey should build a good house probably what is now 28 Christchurch Street East. After Lacey's death his widow married John Newbolt a cardboard maker who died in 1811. In 1786 the premises were assigned to John Singer. In 1792 Ann Lacey, who became Mrs Hiscocks, her stepfather John Newbolt, and John Douglas Middleton, (c. 1757-1829) a carrier, assigned to James Sims a wheelwright. Later the lease was in the names of JD Middleton, his son Stephen, (c.1786-1843) and his daughter Elizabeth, (c.1800-1842) who became Mrs Ware. In 1836 they assigned the lease to Thomas Charles, gent who died in 1851 but the actual occupier was Thomas Bridle from 1836 or earlier until after 1863. By 1878 the block had passed to William Hunt a corn and cider merchant who was still there in 1872 but by 1876 he had given place to John Vallis the builder.

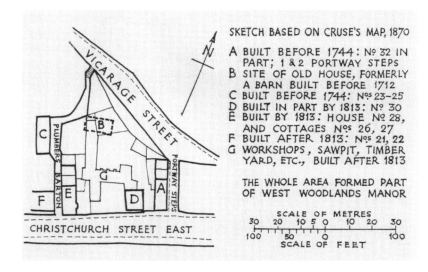

SKETCH BASED ON CRUSE'S MAP, 1870

A BUILT BEFORE 1744 : Nº 32 IN PART; 1 & 2 PORTWAY STEPS
B SITE OF OLD HOUSE, FORMERLY A BARN BUILT BEFORE 1712
C BUILT BEFORE 1744: Nºs 23-25
D BUILT IN PART BY 1813: Nº 30
E BUILT BY 1813: HOUSE Nº 28, AND COTTAGES Nºs 26, 27
F BUILT AFTER 1813: Nºs 21, 22
G WORKSHOPS, SAWPIT, TIMBER YARD, ETC., BUILT AFTER 1813

THE WHOLE AREA FORMED PART OF WEST WOODLANDS MANOR

CHRISTCHURCH STREET EAST

SCALE OF METRES
30   20   10 5 0   10   20   30
100   50   0   100
SCALE OF FEET

Acknowledgements
My particular thanks go to Michael McGarvie FSA who very kindly provided much basic material and the clues for further research. The details from earlier documents are reproduced by courtesy of the Marquis of Bath to whom I express my gratitude as well as to his librarian Miss BM Austin. I am also obliged to the staff of the Wiltshire Record Office and Frome Public Library.

Editor's note
Dr John Hooper Harvey moved to Frome in 1975 and became a national authority on mediaeval architecture and history. He produced a large number of books on the subject including, *The Plantagenets,*1948 *English Medieval Architects* 1954, *The Black Prince and his Age,*1976 & *The Perpendicular Style* 1978. He was a member of the Frome Society and died in no.32 the house that he had so thoroughly researched in 1997. This article appeared originally in the January 1977 edition of the Frome Society newssheet, *Contact.*

THE TICHBORNE CLAIMANT'S VISIT TO FROME 1885

ALM

Two of the most sensational trials of the mid-Victorian period concerned the case of The Tichborne Claimant, made into a film in 1999. The 'Claimant,' otherwise known as Arthur Orton or Thomas Castro was born in Wapping in 1834. He trained as a butcher, joined the merchant service and deserted his ship in South America in 1849. In 1851 he returned to England and then emigrated to Australia in 1853.

The Claimant in 1872

Sir Roger Tichborne, member of a wealthy Hampshire family was born in 1829. He was presumed to have drowned in 1854 after the ship on which he was a passenger sank en route to South America. Sir Roger's mother, the Dowager Lady Tichborne refused to believe her son was dead and made strenuous efforts to find him including placing advertisements in the Australian newspapers.

Thomas Castro, as Orton now called himself, saw the advert and came to England in 1866 to claim the title. The Dowager accepted Castro as her son, but most members of her family did not. After her death in 1868 the Claimant went to court to prove his case. He lost the civil case, which lasted 102 days, and was charged with perjury. In the second trial, which lasted 188 days he was found guilty and sentenced to 14 years penal servitude. He served 10 years 6 months and was released in October 1884. Before his prison sentence he weighed 25 stone, on his discharge he weighed 10 stone!

Following his discharge from prison he accepted an offer of 100 guineas a week to tour the country for one year, lecturing and appearing in music halls and circuses. In 1886 he went to America but the visit was not a success. In 1895 he confessed in newspaper articles that he was Arthur Orton in return for a fee, but later declared that the confession was made only in order to get money. He died destitute in 1898 and a crowd estimated at 5,000 lined the route of his funeral procession.

THE 'TICHBORNE CLAIMANT' AT THE MARKET HALL

From: The Somerset & Wilts Journal 6th June 1885

About 200 people were attracted. to the market hall on Thursday evening last to hear the released convict who still poses as 'Sir Roger Charles Doughty Tichborne, Baronet,' deliver an address on his supposed wrongs. He was appropriately accompanied by a comic female singer who boasted in the name of Miss Nellie Rosamond, and who, in a gentleman's evening attire, sang a characteristic song in music-hall style and then indulged in a dance. The lecturer of the evening was then introduced as 'Sir Roger Tichborne, the Claimant,' by the pianist, who also performed a kind of fantasia on 'Rule Britannia.'

In a style redolent of the genuine Cockney and ex-Wapping butcher he discoursed for upwards of an hour upon his two trials in the Court of Common Pleas and at Bar. He said that his object in appearing before that audience was to get the Act of Parliament, passed in 1878 (declaring him to be an outlaw and dead) repealed, and that they might support him in demanding a Royal Commission of inquiry into his case. Although he intended to bring the most serious charges against those in high position, he reminded the meeting that if those charges were false he would not be allowed to make them again, for there were those only too anxious to lay hold of him once more if they could possibly do so.

He then referred to the great length and cost of his first trial ; tried to account for his erroneous statements about Stonyhurst; denounced the present Lord Chief Justice of England for the means he adopted as Solicitor-General to secure his conviction; read extracts from the evidence and commented thereon, also a letter he sent to Mr Gladstone and the Lord Chancellor in 1873 charging Sir John Coleridge with being guilty of a crime of great magnitude, and protesting against his appointment as Lord Chief Justice, which Mr. Gladstone never condescended to answer; and made charges of the wildest character against the late Mr. Justice Bovill, Serjeant Ballantyne, Mrs Jury, Mr Hopwood, Mrs McAllister, Mary Ann Loader, and the Scotland-yard Detectives, who, he asserted, packed the jury by those who were known to disbelieve his claims. Even the newspapers combined against him not to give fair reports of his meetings. He was subjected to repeated interruptions by one or two individuals and occasional comments of a sympathetic kind from others. At the close he was greeted with applause and the pianist executed "God save the Queen" as a *finale*.

MARKET HALL, FROME.

THURSDAY, JUNE 4th.

THE CLAIMANT,

SIR ROGER CHARLES DOUGHTY TICHBORNE,
WILL give an INTERESTING DISCOURSE UPON HIS LATE TRIAL, Notes from the Detectives and others, also startling facts connected with HIS CONVICTION ! Assisted by

MISS NELLIE ROSAMOND,

THE GREAT CHARACTER VOCALIST.

Doors open at Half-past SEVEN ; commence at EIGHT o'clock. [4533
ADMISSION : Reserved Seats, 1s. ; Promenade, 6d.

THE BLACK DOG INN, STANDERWICK.

A Georgian coaching inn

Mick Davis

The origins of the Black Dog Inn have yet to be traced but they must lie before 1752 as the 'Black Dog Turnpike Trust' a toll road between Bath and Warminster, now the A36, is said to have been named after the pub where the engineers and entrepreneurs held regular meetings. The trust's main responsibilities were the roads leading south from Bath towards Warminster with a branch from Frome and including coal carrying traffic. Going back further it is possible that the inn's name came from the arms of the landowners- the Stourton family which features a 'sea-dog', an odd creature with scales, webbed feet and a broad tail but most definitely black or sable in heraldic parlance. This dog would also have given its name to the nearby Black Dog Woods and Black Dog Farm.

The arms of the Stourton Family[1]

The turnpike trust was set up following an Act of Parliament in 1751 (25 Geo2 c12) and its first mention in print comes from the *Bath Chronicle* of 18 May 1780 which gives notice that the next meeting was to be held on the 23rd. Notices of regular meetings at the inn occur in the newspapers until 1826.

A bankruptcy hearing reported in the *Bath Chronicle* of 14 June 1787 advertises the hearing of a linen draper named Hotchkin who was called to surrender himself at the house of Mrs Grant, Black Dog Inn, Standerwick Common. This is the first name that we have linked to the inn and Mrs Grant was presumably a widow and the mother of William Grant. He married Fanny Moger aged 28 on 26 June 1787 in the parish church at Woolverton, daughter of a 'respectable farmer.' In May 1797 an auction of, 'All those valuable and extensive Woodlands called the Black Dog Woods', was put up for auction at the pub by a Mr John Grant and it seems that the family had extensive interests in the timber industry as well as the inn. Barfoot & Wilkes *Universal British Directory* for 1793-98 lists William Grant as the freeholder of the Black Dog Inn, Westbury under 'Gentry.'

The pub remained in the hands of the Grant family and in 1802 William Grant of the Black Dog offered a reward for the return of a stolen horse and between 1807 and 1811 there were auctions of road tolls 'at the house of William Grant.' The auctions continued until at least 1815 but Grant is not mentioned after1813 and it is likely that someone else had taken over as landlord.

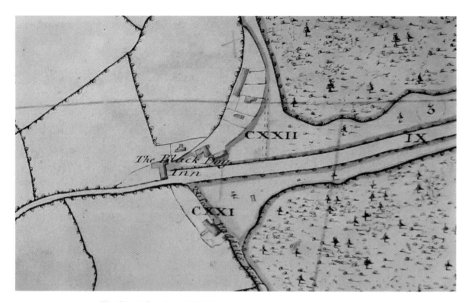

The Black Dog Inn, 1808 Enclosure Map (Warminster Museum)

Jeremiah Cruse the much-neglected surveyor and cartographer held a meeting at the pub on 6 June 1816 as the Commissioner named in an Act of Parliament entitled, *'An Act for enclosing lands within the parishes is of Berkeley and Somerset.'* At this meeting various local landowners where encouraged to exchange various plots of land or buildings with each other to rationalise their holdings. Cruse would then 'allot and award such exchanges' under the terms of the act.

On 3 January 1817 Fanny Grant died at Old Dilton, about four miles away, aged 58 and on 13 January the pub was advertised for sale or rent but was still on the market in March. It sold eventually because in March 1819 William Grant senior, aged 61 a timber merchant and churchwarden of Standerwick Common described as 'formally of the Black Dog Inn' was walking in a water meadow when he fell into a ditch and drowned. On 25 February of the following year his estate, which included land, houses and buildings in Westbury Parish was put up for auction as detailed in the *Salisbury & Winchester Journal* for 7 February 1820.

It can be assumed that the purchaser of the Black Dog in 1817 was a William Barter described as a brewer, chapman and dealer of Frome and it was during his tenure that one of the pub's most infamous events took place.

On 24 February of that year a minor aristocrat, Thomas Champneys master of Orchardleigh Park a large estate and mansion house just outside Frome, arrived with his servant George Higgins. Champneys was in hiding. Although heir to vast estates he was also heir to even bigger debts which his profligate behaviour had done nothing to reduce. There were many warrants out for his arrest for debt an imprisonable offence at that time.

48

Two of the many warrants against him were enforceable only within the county of Somerset and Champneys sought to buy time by hiding just over the county line in Wiltshire while his lawyers attempted to sort the matter out. Unfortunately for him word of his whereabouts had been leaked and his arch enemies, the Messiters, lawyers and bankers of Frome were hot on his trail. They had spent some time buying up all his small debts in the town and guaranteeing his bail which gave them almost unlimited rights over his personal freedom. They could withdraw bail at any time and have him imprisoned until all these debts had been settled.

Champneys was sitting at his desk in the Black Dog awaiting his dinner when the Messiters burst in. He received them civilly knowing that he had no choice but to comply with their requests and received a promise from them that they were taking him to London to appear in front of the King's Bench which would not have resulted in his imprisonment. Contemporary accounts detail the events-

On this understanding Champneys entered the chaise which had been procured from Frome and the driver was told to set his horses heads towards Warminster, but as soon as Mr Champneys was secured, to drive as hard as possible for two miles on the Frome Road. Mr Champneys was accompanied in the carriage by Thomas Ivey, the sheriff's officer and all proceeded quietly until the horses were suddenly turned around towards Frome, and the plaintiff, seeing how he had been deceived put his hand upon George Messiter's shoulder and said "You traitor you have entrapped and deceived me; how can I take your word again as a gentleman?" Champneys entreated Messiter to return:

but his plea met with no other reply than the appearance of a drawn dagger and a threat of applying its powers.

Maddened, the plaintiff reached across to the door next to the bailiff and in so doing kicked a box containing his possessions against it causing it to fall into the road and smash. The next state in which the plaintiff was found was that of being half out of the carriage exclaiming *Murder!* The horses were by now in full gallop and he was dragged till the cries of the bailiff who did not lease his hold, were added to those of the plaintiff, causing the carriage to stop. When it had done so the bailiff loosened his fingers and Champneys fell to the ground being immediately seized and struck a violent blow with a cudgel on his head which caused him to stagger but fortunately only demolished his hat. Force was then used to drag him once more to the carriage, but he absolutely refused unless his box, in which was a valuable gold watch and £50 in cash, was given to him. This Nathaniel Messiter refused crying, "Drag him along, the scoundrel, drag him along, I have pistols and will use them!"

The more humane bailiff, Mr Ivey, advised Champneys to get into the carriage again upon being promised that his box should be restored. Champneys got in and the party travelled until they got within about half a mile of the county of Somerset where they were met by Sheriff Williamson who enquired if Squire Champneys was in the carriage?" "Oh yes", replied George Messiter, "he is here". Sherriff Williamson had been part of the plot against the plaintiff and was waiting to arrest him having received the warrants at the Black Dog earlier in the evening unseen by Champneys. He proceeded to take the plaintiff in execution upon those very writs which George Messiter had vowed to God should not be executed and the party arrived at the George Inn at Frome.

Mr Champneys, under these circumstances, was thrown into a violent fever and although there was no sign of violence upon his person he was confined to his bed for several days and required the attendance of a medical person being bruised and hardly able to walk. During that time he was locked in his room at the George with Ivey and Williamson in a room adjoining. At the end of five days he was released from his bail upon his solicitor, Mr Evill of Bath joining in a bond of indemnity to Nathaniel Messiter and was able to discharge the writs.[2]

The Black Dog's connection to Thomas Champneys was not to end yet however. He took the Messiters to court for false imprisonment later in the year and won but in the meantime they had been spreading rumours around Frome that Champneys had been making homosexual advances to some of his tenants and others in the town. Champneys took George Messiter to court once more charging him with slander. One of the witnesses for the Messiter's defence was the landlord William Barter. Champneys won again.

In 1826 Barter was declared bankrupt and the inn put up for auction in September of the following year. The property was described as having a brew house, stables, coach house, granary, courtyard and garden then in the occupation of a Mr Bown as a yearly tenant. The successful bidder was a Thomas Axford of Tytherington who paid £605.

Like many pubs at the time the Black Dog was the venue for coroner's inquests with the deceased often laid out in a back room for the jury to inspect. By a strange coincidence, the body in question on 17 December 1832 was that of Thomas Ford a weaver of Short Street, Chapmanslade. Ford had been set upon, beaten up and died shortly after the election riots occasioned by the contest between Thomas Champneys and Thomas Sheppard in Frome Marketplace. If Champneys was aware of the inquest it must have brought back memories of the time he was kidnapped there many years before. The jury returned a verdict of wilful murder but nobody was ever arrested over the matter.[2]

The house continued to be an important coaching inn on the road from Bath to Warminster for many years holding auctions, functions and inquests as well as meetings and presumably the collection of tolls. In the 1830s it was also the starting point for hunting parties with Mr Codrington's hounds.

Thomas Axford was still there as landlord in the census of 1841 aged 50 with his wife Mary three sons and five servants described as a publican and the inn as on the Bath Road, Westbury. A year later in July of 1842 there was a knock on the door and he was arrested and charged with stealing quantities of oats. The case was brought by a carrier named Atkins who was employed to carry corn on behalf of dealers in Bristol and Warminster. There were many complaints that when the corn arrived at its destination there was less of it than there had been when its journey began. An investigation revealed that the odd sack of corn had been taken by Henry Pond the 19-year-old ostler on behalf of his employer Thomas Axford. Pond confessed and turned King's Evidence but failed to appear at the trial which collapsed as a result.

It seems that Axford did not survive the scandal for long as in March of 1846 the freehold of the 'old established and well accustomed inn' was put up for auction on the premises 'comprising every convenience for carrying on an extensive business, now in full trade', the sitting tenant, and presumably landlord, was a Mr George Hoddinott who must have taken over from Axford sometime previously. Hoddinott went bankrupt in the early part of 1848 and his entire stock in trade including brewing plant, beer, spirits, beer engine, carthorse and even his household furniture was auctioned on 20 March of that year. Once his tenure at the Black Dog came to an end he was described as a haulier, dealer in coal & coke and small farmer, late of Short Street in Westbury Leigh.

The census of 1851 lists Joseph Maundrell aged 52, inn keeper, his wife Harriet Taylor and two children. Little has been discovered about his time at the inn but he was born at Rodden near Frome in 1798 and described as a woollen weaver there in 1841. In 1858 after his time at the Black Dog he is listed on the electoral roll as owning a house and land at Standerwick and in the census of 1861 he has become an inn keeper and a farmer of 34 acres, no pub is named but it is almost certainly the newly built Bell just across the road. The first mention of this pub is the report of an inquest held there in 1860 and it does not appear on the 1851 census so quite possibly Maundrell moved across the road as its first landlord. By 1871 he had retired and was lodging with his sister in law Elizabeth Taylor at the Three Horse Shoes Inn, Bradford on Avon, he died the same year aged 73.

Back at the Black Dog, by 1857 James Davis and family are running the show and in the 1861 census he was aged 34 and there with his wife Martha and two children aged five and three both born in Standerwick. George Davis 32, a wheelwright and carpenter presumably a brother, carries on his trade from the same area. James left in April of 1873 auctioning off his entire stock down to the beds, clocks and spittoons; possibly the competition from the new pub was too much. By 1881 Thomas Taylor and family had taken over, he was a baker and beer seller with wife Sarah listed as assistant baker and possibly hoping to make a living from baking rather than just beer. Taylor died in 1885 and the licence passed to his wife who continued until 1888 when it passed to Charles Millard after having been advertised as, 'The Black Dog Beer House with baking and grocery business attached, apply to the Bath Arms Brewery, Frome'. This business was owned by the Baily family who had many brewing and pub interests in that town.

Charles and Alice Millard were still there in 1893 as innkeeper, grocer and baker but the following year the pub was once more up for rent as a 'good baking business' and soon taken by George Cornish. His tenure does not seem to have been very successful as when the tenancy moved to Charles Henry Meech in 1898 it was described as having been 'closed for some time' and the following year it passed to Edward Dicker, an inn keeper age 59 and his wife Mary who were to prove the last licensees.

The brewing interests of the Baily family were amalgamated with others in 1889 to form the Frome United Breweries Company Ltd who also owned the Bell 126 yards away on the opposite side of the road. At that time there were only 29 houses within a radius of half a mile and a population of about 125, scarcely any business was done at the Black Dog and what trade there was went to the Bell. At a licensing hearing in February 1910 the justices decided that its continuing license was unnecessary and the owners agreed. It was a sad end to what had been a very important Georgian coaching inn full of the hustle and bustle of commerce, the changing of horses and travellers staying overnight waiting to continue their journey the following day, of meetings, auctions and inquests, food, drink and merry banter. On 29 June 1911 the freehold was auctioned as a 12 roomed dwelling house with cart shed garden and WC at the rear with a good bakehouse and a brick oven included in the sale. There were no takers on this occasion and once the building had reached £165 it was withdrawn but sold after the auction to Mr F Moore.

Whether Moore lived in it or rented it we do not know, in fact we know nothing further until August 1940 when John Coles, the Frome auctioneer, had the property up for sale. It had been renamed 'The Pantiles' and was sold prior to the auction itself. The purchaser was (eventually) Major General John Sydney Lethbridge. His daughter, Nemone, spent part of her childhood there and the ancient walls were loved once more,

> the house, which dated in part from the 16th century was built of blocks of local stone plastered and then white washed, the roof was made of moss-grown pantiles which replaced the original thatch. To this structure was added two farm labourers cottages forming together a long thin house never more than one room wide in the shape of the letter L. The foot of the L was what was known as the stillroom a long low building one story high with slate lined shelves which must have been used for brewing and storing beer when the house was a coaching inn. There was a large neglected garden, a paddock with a muddy pond and an orchard full of old-fashioned apple trees, the Morgan Sweet, Tom Put and Sheep's Nose the fruit of which are never seen on a supermarket shelf.
> The surrounding countryside was an idyllic playground there was lush Meadowland grazed by short red shorthorn cattle dotted with great freestanding elms and small coppices which gave shelter to pheasants and innumerable songbirds. When we walked quietly there at night we could hear nightjars and nightingales. There was the river Frome with its glass clear tributaries where we collected tadpoles and portal stickleback with pollarded willows by the water's edge.

The family had always been keen to be part of the community and in 1942 started the Standerwick branch of the Women's Institute which met at the cottage with Mrs Lethbridge as secretary. At the beginning of 1950 representatives of all three political parties were invited to the cottage to address a crowded drawing room and one year later Miss Nemone Lethbridge was elected secretary of the Wells Division of the Young Liberal Association. After 10 years the family was relieved of the burden of holding meetings in their living room and the Women's Institute had its own hut erected at Rudge. In one of the cottages next door lived a Mrs Axford wife of Horace who came to work for the family- he was almost certainly a descendant from the landlord from 100 years before.

In December 1960 Major General Lethbridge put the Black Dog up for sale described as a 'charming period house and old coaching inn with a delightful garden and land of two acres with four bedrooms and outbuildings adjoining.'

The family moved to Devon and Nemone moved to London where she trained as a barrister being called to the Bar in 1956 - one of the first women barristers. She focused on crime and became the only female tenant at 3 Harcourt Buildings. Undaunted by the clerks' refusal to give her work, she found her own and her considerable reputation was made when she became counsel of choice to the Krays.

A young Nemone, seated, with, grandmother Lady Maynard, sister Cherry & Cellophane the rabbit in the garden at Black Dog Cottage

After only a few years of practice, her tenancy was summarily terminated when news of her marriage to Jimmy O'Connor, who had been convicted of murder and narrowly escaped the death penalty, became public. During the 18 years it took her to return practising law she wrote successful television plays as did her husband Jimmy, she retired in 2007.

The Black Dog in 1987

[1] I am grateful to Michael McGarvie for this suggestion
[2] The full story of Sir Thomas Champneys is told in 'A Surfeit of Magnificence'. The Trials & Tribulations of Sir Thomas Champneys of Orchardleigh by Mick Davis and published by the Hobnob Press.
[3] I am very grateful to Nemone Lethbridge and Milo O'Connor for permission to quote from their book, Nemone, and the use of their family photos.

53

FOOD FOR THOUGHT

J D Wainwright

This charming roundup of eateries around Frome comes from *The Blue House Restored* a pamphlet published in 1965 in support of the restoration work to be carried out on that historic almshouse.

'Truffles, according to Peter Dominic's, *Wine Mine,* used to be found in the forests of Epping and Savernake. Surely in our area there must be a corner of Selwood Forest where these might still be unearthed. Here lies an opportunity for the owner of a properly trained pig or Bassett hound to provide himself with a profit and a purveyor of food with a highly valued and sought-after specialty. Delicacies of this kind lead inevitably to thoughts of haute cuisine, but it is not the intention here to tempt readers' palates to such heights. Even if one could afford it, there's no point in approaching the condition of Pierette, (sister of Brillat-Savarin) who, towards the end of a monumental repast, cried, "Quickly! Pass me the desert, I think I'm going to die".

The scope of this article has in the main been limited to personal experience, but in some cases reports from friends interested in gastronomy have had to be relied upon. A realisation that miles of motoring will be as equally unpleasant as planning a meal, eating it and later washing up, has limited the choice of places to those who can be reached within about 15 to 30 minutes driving time from Frome. Omissions from the selection does not mean that equally excellent establishments do not exist; undoubtedly more hidden culinary art will come to light as the trend towards providing wider ranges of better food and beverages of every sort gains further momentum. There would be no purpose either in trying to emulate Egon Ronay or any other author of a good food guide, and for this reason no attempt has been made at the classification either for quality of food or price consideration.

Within the driving times suggested one can reach from Frome the incomparable Hole in the Wall at Bath, or if Mendip weather conditions permit, easily drive to the Crown Hotel at

An early postcard of the Portway Hotel

Wells, where the high and unvarying standard should not pass unrecognised. If one has a very fast car a somewhat lengthier dash across the Mendips will bring one to the Mendip Hotel at Blagdon where the view is breathtaking and lavish appointments keep company with a very comprehensive menu; or to the less distant Miner's Arms where Mendip snails make an interesting prélude to a meal splendidly prepared and served.

In the town itself is the Portway Hotel with its unusual but pleasing pate as one favourite, and where hidden among other interesting wines is No 32 a Pouilly Blanc Fumee. The local Mendip Motel I am told, is tempting diners with *caneton Montmorency;* but these establishments are so well known that it would be pointless to describe their cooking once again –or to enlarge upon the facilities offered by the George Hotel which is the traditional focal point for so many local functions.

The Mendip Lodge Motel, now housing.

With a couple of gallons of petrol in the tank of an average car and £2 in the handbag or wallet, any reader ought to be able to go out to lunch or supper and come home after a pleasing eating experience with some small change. On the other hand, the extravagance of a whole bottle of wine will probably need an extra note. Among the places mentioned are those which provide a pleasant fresh meal from three shillings upward – something of a rarity in these times-and so, being a selfish writer, I shall leave interested readers to seek them out for themselves. At the same time I advise them, when they have decided which places to visit, to concentrate on the lunch hour when they are not so likely to be crowded.

Just over the border in Wiltshire we find the Royal Oak at Corsley. The reason for mentioning this particular pub is that a new bar with eating facilities has recently been added to the old building. Whilst the décor of this extension is modern by comparison, it has been skilfully handled. A varied cold buffet was available when I called and it seems likely that it is going to become a popular spot for getting a meal. Rumour has it that under new management grills are appearing on the menu.

Not far distant is the Three Horseshoes in the pleasant village of Chapmanslade. The interior here is graced by creepers and climbers, such as *philodendron* and *kangaroo vine*. The dishes provided are of the usual cold variety, but hot pies and delicious sausages can also be had if required. Particularly good is the cold ham served with salad. One drawback, if one does not wish to sit at the bar when eating, is that the height of some of the tables is such that it is not easy to get the knees underneath. The bewhiskered landlord will occasionally dispense snuff to such customers as indulge this habit, his range covering the crudest 'blasting powder' to the finest Seville.

Also in Wiltshire and hard by the Longleat estate lies the Bath Arms. Here one may obtain, at the bar at lunchtime, delicious hot soups and pasties plus a variety of cold items including sandwiches. Chicken and chips served in baskets are also 'on'. For an evening meal there is offered an excellent, if in some respects limited menu; the dining room itself is delightfully furnished and the service most efficient. Meals are cooked to order, and so some prior notice of arrival-especially on a Saturday-is advisable though not essential. No meals are served in the dining room on Sunday or Monday evenings. The setting of the Bath Arms alone at the thatched cottage village of Horningsham amid tall trees makes a visit here worthwhile.

Coming back in Somerset one can find a place which must be unique, notably the Full Moon at Rudge. This small and not too easily found inn has some different aspects to offer. It must be one of the rare spots where you can still eat your meal seated at a scrubbed table. Unfortunately, recent redecoration meant that the stone floor of one of the bars has been covered with plastic tiles. However, a great deal of charm still hangs about this establishment. Simple cold meals can be obtained here but they are remarkable in that the butter is rolled into proper balls and is home-made. The bread comes from an old-fashioned bakery and the ingredients for a salad are picked from the garden. By a fortunate accident one of my visits to this place coincided with the strawberry harvest and we were served with these and farm cream. Being a small country inn, I would not recommend a large party to descend without first giving some warning; but if you want a quiet few minutes away from the traffic, this spot must be one of the best.

The Red Lion, Woolverton

Not far away we have the Red Lion at Woolverton already noted by Egon Ronay for quite obvious reasons. The food here is excellent and is very nicely served. Meat when cut from a large joint always seems to taste better than when cut from the smaller one. At the Red Lion where the turnover of food must be considerable, they obviously need large joints and this, I think, together with some expert cooking is probably the reason why the flavour seems to be so good. This, of course, is one of the nearest places where the prawn addict can make himself very much at home, and a little of the interesting pink- coloured mayonnaise can be used to good effect. There is an added attraction which is by no means common, of being able to sit out of doors, when the weather allows, to take your meals.

In Rode, only a few moments' drive from Woolverton we come across the comparatively new Sportsman's Steak House. This enterprise is run on a scale considerably in excess of any of the other places that I am going to mention. Here the architects have combined old and new successfully mixing the air of a restaurant with the features of a barn; this is a place where one can come with the idea of sitting down to a more formal, definitely filling type of meal.

Matchbox Label from the Sportsman in the 1970s

My next choice is the Hungerford Arms at Farleigh Hungerford where we come across expertly produced food, and a speciality in the form of one of the widest selections of ingredients that comprise a salad that I have seen anywhere. It was a cold night when I last visited and my meal was preceded by a delicious game soup with the second helping just as good as the first. From other visitors come high praise for the grills.

On the other side of Frome heading towards the Mendips, we are approaching another string of houses where the food standards are high and specialities exist. Firstly, one encounters the Sun at Whatley with this choice of interesting toasted sandwiches. While these take some minutes to prepare they are both enjoyable and satisfying. Soups and other dishes can be obtained too, and you can eat out of doors if you wish. Another unusual facility is the telephone on the bar. Perhaps the nervous should be warned that there are quarries nearby and blasting at certain times causes audible distractions.

Continuing in the direction of Maesbury Ring along on a road which for some extraordinary reason is not marked in the AA Handbook, one finds the lovely Wagon and Horses. Visually the exterior of this house is one of the most pleasing to me, and under the new management the face of the interior is also being considerably altered. Here a speciality available at all times is 'Chicken in the Rough'. This is simply a portion of cold chicken with a small cottage type roll and butter. The secret lies in the cooking, and I can only discover that the ingredient that makes the difference would be found in the French cookery book. What is more unexpected is that from Monday to Friday you can obtain grills here and it is also the only inn that I know where you can buy an omelette. Soups are added to the menu in the winter, and this may appear to be most necessary when one considers the inn's exposed position.

For some reason Shepton Mallet looks like turning into a gastronomic centre and competition is obviously going to be fierce, so one should be able to look forward to obtaining meals of considerable variety and quality in any one of the three fairly recently opened dining rooms. The nearest one to Frome is the Charlton House Hotel where the inventor of Ilchester Cheese has modernised a delightful small country house standing in a most attractive position with a fine lawn sweeping down to the dining room windows. This is one place that I have not yet visited personally but I have received a report of the finest steak that a friend has ever eaten. In addition to this it must deserve a special mention as it is the only restaurant that I know where Galeeny has appeared on the menu.

In another part of Shepton Mallet we come across the King's Arms known locally as the 'Dust Hole'. Renovations have resulted in the construction of a dining room with its own small cocktail bar. My first meal began with a terrine of duck and went on to include some very tender veal. The menu, modestly called the Bill of Fare is extensive and here again one can look forward to food carefully prepared and beautifully cooked. In the bar one has a remarkable choice of 101 sandwiches hot, cold, open or shut. As can be imagined some of these are unconventional and I quote the ingredients of one known as, 'Mum's Special' which comprises:

A toasted sandwich filled with crab and grated cheese bound with salad dressing on curry paste and butter spread.

Last, but by no means least, is the third new eating place in Shepton Mallet and this is Bowlish House. As you leave the town on the road for Wells you will pass this handsome building now carefully restored, on your left-hand side where the road drops down into the valley. An uncommon but promising feature is a charcoal grill and whilst a visit has not yet been made the omens are that we can look forward to something exceptional.

I trust that interested people will now go out and explore these places where one can experience meals that are 'pleasing to the palate soothing to the stomach and gratifying withal'.

Social Comment: Button Bridge 2013

Mendip Council 1974 - 2023

FROME BUILDINGS 25: INNOX HILL HOUSE

Antiquarius

Despite the destruction during the 1960s Frome still has a fine selection of Georgian buildings and one of the least known is Innox Hill House high on a hill overlooking Welshmill and the town. Its origins are uncertain but it seems to have been constructed by a 'Mr Grant' slightly before 1800 and its owner would appear to have been John Vincent a surgeon and apothecary of Frome who married Elizabeth Edgell of Standerwick on 25 July 1771. In 1784 he sold the leases on some property, possibly to finance the building of his new mansion. The first mention connecting Vincent to the house occurs in 1800 when his younger daughter Mary Ann Vincent of Innox Hill marries Captain Richard James Lawrence O'Connor of the Royal Navy.

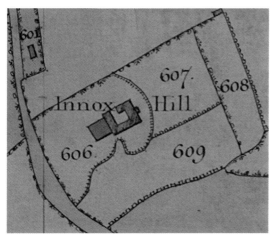

John Vincent died in Paris in 1811 leaving the house to his wife Elizabeth. The property is shown on the Cruse map of 1813 as in her ownership and occupation. Its form is pretty much as it is today with the main house in red and a range of out buildings and stables attached.

On 23 March 1818 the house and grounds were advertised for rent in the local paper with a detailed description:

A COMPLETE FAMILY RESIDENCE AND LANDS

To be Let, either furnished or unfurnished, for a term of years, with immediate possession. The spacious and very desirable MANSION, called INNOX-HILL HOUSE with numerous domestic offices, stabling, double coach house, walled garden lawn and plantations and surrounded with about 17 acres of excellent land, beautifully situated about half a mile from Frome. The house is modern and in the most perfect state of repair: on the ground floor are lofty dining and drawing rooms of large dimensions with breakfast room and parlour; the principle staircase leads from the vestibule to five very superior bedrooms with convenient closets over which are four excellent sleeping rooms and large closets approached by the back staircase; the basement comprises a spacious servants hall, large kitchen (replete with every necessary appendage), china closet, pantry, wine and beer cellars, boot room and wash house; a spacious enclosed curtilage leads to stables for six horses, double coach house, coal and wood houses and other necessary buildings. The garden lies at the back of the premises adjoining to which are a barn, cow shed and piggery. The lands are of the finest quality and most eligibly arranged around the house, the entrance to which leads from the turnpike road through a plantation by the lawn. The situation is delightful, commanding beautiful prospects of the extensive surrounding country and the neighbourhood very respectable. A good family pew in the parish church.

For other particulars and renting apply to Messrs. Crocker at their Land Agency Office, Frome who will issue cards for viewing.

The estate was still being advertised for rent the following September and there is no record to say if it was tenanted or otherwise. The churchwarden's accounts for 1822 to 1826 show Captain O'Connor as paying the rates. O'Connor died in 1826 at the age of 56 and was described as being of Innox Hill House and Carrickfoyle in Jamaica where estates producing sugar and rum had been in the O'Connor family since at least the 1770s.

In March of 1829 there is yet another advertisement for the property to be rented but again no indication as to whether tenants were found but Pigot's Directory of 1830 gives Mrs O'Connor, 'gentry' as owner.

In June 1835 Elizabeth Vincent eldest daughter of the late Captain Richard JL O'Connor RN married Lieut. Colonel John William Aitcheson of the East India Company's Service. We are on firmer ground when the census begins in 1841 with the house being shown as occupied by John Aitcheson aged 45 of the Indian Army, his wife Eliza aged 35, their three daughters and six servants. Quite possibly they were renting the house from Elizabeth Vincent, the widow of John Vincent the original builder now aged 69. The house seems to have been shared with their relatives as Mary Ann O'Connor is recorded as dying in the house in 1846 at the age of 74.

John Aitcheson died in Bath in 1847 at the age of 54 and the following year Elizabeth Vincent is shown as paying the rates once more and by the census of 1851 she is back in the house listed as a 'Landed Proprietor' aged 78. Also listed are Mary Ann Reid O'Connor her niece aged 46 and grandaughter Isabella Eliza O'Connor born in India and aged 21. The house servants have now been reduced to three.

By 1860 the house was occupied by Dr Thomas Sunderland Harrison aged 60 with a distinguished medical career. He was a member of The Royal Medical & Chirurgical Society

trained in Edinburgh and qualifying in 1834 a former lecturer in midwifery at the Charlotte School of Medicine in London and Senior physician at the Farringdon Dispensary, London. Born in Lancashire, Harrison sat as a Somerset magistrate. He is listed at Innox Hill in the Medical Directory for that year as well as having a house at 3 Portland Place, Bath. This was yet another residency secured by marriage as his wife Catherine Lawrence O'Connor was a niece of Elizabeth Vincent and daughter of Richard O'Connor. Harrison died

Innox Hill House in 2010

in 1864 she died in 1869. The pair had previously lived at Garston Lodge in Frome having married in 1850. Harrison was a widower 1861 Elizabeth Vincent is still there aged 88. The grand matriarch died in 1869 at the age of 97 and the house passes from the family for the first time since it was built over 70 years before. In 1871 it is occupied by Captain James Dolphin late of the Rifle Brigade aged 60, his wife Agnes, daughter Isobel and four servants.

The house had by now acquired a lodge at the bottom of the hill occupied by a Thomas Maggs a coachman and his family. Captain Dolphin was not to enjoy the property for very long as an auction of his furniture and effects was arranged for 24 September 1874 as he was 'leaving the premises and removing to a distance'. In fact, he removed further than he expected as by the end of the month he was dead. There are two versions of this event, the first states that while pursuing a wasp he broke a pane of glass and cut his thumb whereupon tetanus set in causing his death; the second version is that he caught a severe cold while in Weymouth which resulted in inflammation and congestion of the lungs from which he died. He was described as highly respected, of a genial disposition and an active campaigner for the Conservative Party. His widow was still there at the end of the year when she organised the collection of Christmas presents for the Frome Union Workhouse.

The entrance hall and staircase to no.37

The next occupant was Joseph Parsons, wife Fanny and three daughters. Parsons was a retired nickel plater from Wells and the long chain of military and medical men was at last broken. Parsons died in around 1886 and the house was put up for auction on 17 June of that year by Harding and Sons who described it as 'almost unrivalled for the beauty of its location, and within an enclosure of 13 acres. Whether it sold or not is not recorded but, on the 9 September Mrs Parsons auctioned off most of its contents in over 200 lots as she was leaving the neighbourhood. Harding & Sons records, detailing every item and the amount raised is now in the library at Frome Museum. From nickel plating we move on to brewing, the next occupant being Jonathan Drew Knight and family who were there for the 1891 census. He had previously been at Christchurch Street working as a 'master brewer' employing ten men. Knight married Emma Jane Mees the daughter of William Mees the proprietor of the Crown Hotel in the Market Place. Mees was already a widower by 1851 and his other daughter Mary Ann married Frances James Knight – both sons of William Knight who kept the Castle Inn on Catherine Hill and the brewery behind it. The family are still there in 1901 with Jonathan now 63 years of age and still active as a brewer and employer. He died at the house on 17 June 1907 aged 69.

The 20th century was not kind to the once proud Georgian house. Details are increasingly hard to come by as its inhabitants become less notable and details from census returns are unavailable after 1911. By the census of that year the house was occupied by Thomas George Sargeant and his wife Georgina he was 67 and a retired policeman from Bath. He was described as a house caretaker and it seems that the couple were installed just to look after the 15-room mansion.

Nothing has been discovered about the house and its occupiers between the wars but at some point probably just before the war the building was split vertically into two houses numbered as 36 and 37 Innox Hill. During 1943 no.36, which is the half on the left hand side as you look at the front, was occupied by Mr DW Humphries who seems to have been involved in various sporting events for young people in the town as well as being active in the 'China Campaign Committee'. On 23 March 1949 Humphreys put number 36 up for auction at the George in Frome. Bids opened at £2000 and was finally sold for £3000 to a Mr MA Stevens. The property at this time, comprised about one third of the total building, and consisted of two reception rooms with four bedrooms with a small grass paddock with outbuildings.

On 20 October 1965 36 was back in the auction room this time advertised with one and a quarter acre with outline planning permission for a new building and the possibility of conversion into flats which was applied for in 1971 by a Commander AS Craig. In more recent times the four flats were tenanted by a housing association before being sold and are now in the process of being converted back into one residence.

The larger side of the building, number 37 was occupied by Cyril Mitchell managing director of Messrs. Wallington Weston Ltd and his wife Marion from at least 1942. It was Mitchell who converted 37 into its present three flats in 1955. He died in 1985 and his address was given as The Mews, Hill House, a flat built above the old stable block. The situation remains the same today with various plots sold off for the construction of large contemporary properties and 37 divided into three spacious flats.

Obituary, 1784. April 23. Was found dead, in his house at Frome, William Thatcher, an old man, who for many years past had subsisted on the charitable benefactions of his neighbours. His success in the begging trade was considerable, as may be perceived by the following inventory of property found in his house at his death: 22*l*. in silver, 2 guineas in gold; 5*l*. in copper, 12 old hats, 14 pair of shoes, 14 pair of stockings, 35 cakes, 2 bushels of morsels of bread, cheese, flesh, &c., &c.—The above has not been long accumulating; for but two years since his house was robbed of the valuables it then contained, which were much more considerable than the above.—*The Gentleman's Magazine*.

BELGIAN REFUGEES IN FROME DURING WORLD WAR 1

Liz Corfield

As one of the guarantors – alongside France and Germany – of the 1839 Treaty of London, Britain was honour bound to recognise and protect Belgium's independence and neutrality. When Germany invaded in 1914 it was obliged to step in and deal with one of the major effects of the Great War - the large displacement of population. At least 250,000 Belgian citizens took refuge in Britain during the course of the war.

Frome began preparing for an influx of Belgian refugees in September 1914. A national War Refugees Committee (WRC) had been established to source accommodation for those who had fled the country and Frome was one of 2,500 places nationwide that set up a sub-committee to deal with the situation. It was just as well that action was taken speedily because on 14 October 1914, 16,000 refugees arrived at Folkestone in one day. Initially the Belgians had travelled privately but now a service of steamers was provided from Le Havre.

Belgian refugees bound for Folkestone

Photo credit to Alan F Taylor

Belgian refugees arriving at Folkestone

Photo credit to Alan F Taylor

The Duchess of Somerset, a leading light on the WRC, gave a rousing speech in Frome at the beginning of September and it was announced at this meeting that 120 offers of homes to accommodate 162 persons had already been received and that those residents on the list were quite prepared to support the refugees from their own pocket. A motion was passed that 50 refugees be sent to Frome initially and the committee would judge whether the town was in a position to take more. Two sub committees were set up, one of hospitality, members of which should speak French, and one for the reception of the refugees in the town. A house to house collection was organised to help fund the needs of the Belgians.

The very first refugees, 11 adults and one child, arrived in Frome on Saturday 5 September 1914, followed by five more on Sunday. They were reported as 'looking worn and sad' and belonged 'to the middle class'. One lady, Mme Oorts, was diagnosed with appendicitis a day after her arrival in Frome. She had only been married for five weeks and had to flee her home town of Louvain, leaving all her worldly possessions behind. She was operated upon at Victoria Hospital and subsequently made a full recovery. Her husband, Mons Oorts, a corresponding clerk, spoke a little English, and had been rejected as unfit by the Belgian Army. He and his wife were lodged with Rev Arnold Cook at Fromefield with another refugee, Mons Lecerf of Antwerp, a hairdresser, who spoke some English. Mons Oorts was interviewed by the local newspaper and was able to give an idea of the difficulties they had faced in leaving Belgium, quitting the house which he had just purchased and all its contents and fleeing with just the clothes they stood up in and some items which could be easily carried. Their first stop from their home town was Antwerp, to his parents' house, but after a couple of weeks he and his wife were given just 24 hours to leave. The town was overcrowded and the Germans were closing in. A siege seemed likely and the authorities were concerned that food might run out. One of the two men who arrived on Wednesday had been forced to march in front of the German Army with his hands held above his head. Twenty-seven more arrived on 18 September and this made up the full complement of 50 which Frome had agreed to take. These were mainly of the 'peasant farmer and cultivator class', with distressing tales to tell of their homes and animals being burned. The Belgians were pleased to be able to attend a service at St Catherine's, where they were welcomed by Dean Lonergan, who was able to speak to them in Flemish and continued to conduct Mass with them every Sunday.

The residents of Frome rose to the challenge of housing the refugees, who were taken into their own homes and in at least two instances had small houses provided for them, at Milk Street and Castle Street - furnished and fitted out rent free. The refugees in these were supported entirely by the committee whilst some others were lodged and boarded at the expense of the committee. This was quite a commitment on the part of Frome residents as there was no way of knowing how long this arrangement might last. Even the Board of Guardians offered 84 beds plus bedding should it be needed.

The thorny question of whether or not the refugees be offered work was raised by the end of the month. It was agreed that work would be beneficial but it was paramount that there was no displacement of local labour so the subject was temporarily shelved, although a memo from WRC pointed out that it was not the 'business of a local committee to act as an employment bureau'. A government commission had been set up to provide for the occupation of Belgian refugees and by April 1915 all but one man living in Frome was in some kind of employment – encouraged by the king of Belgium who stated ,"Do not pauperise my people, do not let them rust in idleness, as I do not want them to become a charge on friendly people". If the refugees became self-supporting then this would relieve the local committee of some pressing financial obligations. Frome supplied munitions for the front and

Belgium was, pre-war, regarded as the premier country for the manufacture of armaments in Europe, so it's likely that Belgian workers helped in their production.

Raising funds and support was always going to be a challenge. Internationally, sacks of flour were sent from Canada to aid the war effort and the sacks were later sold for souvenirs at 5s each, two thirds to the Prince of Wales National Relief Fund and one third to the Belgian Refugees Fund. A ship, the *Doric*, arrived in Plymouth with food, clothing and shoes and boots. A bale of flannel, received by the central committee was distributed with the idea that the refugees would make garments for their army. It was of some solace to the refugees to think they were doing something useful for the war effort. Clothing expenses were particularly high. Weekly expenditure went to those who were not billeted in family homes and the rest was earmarked for clothing, doctors' bills and incidental expenses. Besides money, clothing and foodstuffs were also donated. It was all seen as doing one's bit for the war effort. However, some subscribers said they couldn't afford weekly subscriptions after Christmas and new subscribers would be needed.

Locally, benefit performances were held by the Picture Palace, house to house collections were organised, as were weekly subscriptions. Money raised from performances at the Albany went into the fund, as did entry fees from a dance and the 'gate' at a local football match at Badgers Hill. By 23 October 1914 £142/14/3 had been raised via collections and weekly subscriptions. A Christmas tea, entertainment, games and presents were provided for the refugees including a visit by Father Christmas who seemed to be a novelty to the children. Over 2,000 troops were also billeted in Frome at this time.

Belgian refugee children.

Photo credit to Alan F Taylor

By 16 October Frome had a complement of 55 refugees and this number remained pretty constant over the five years. Not everyone who came to Frome stayed, although it was recognised that the refugees preferred being in town to being in rural or isolated places. Some moved to London and others went back to Belgium to join the army. By December 1914 all refugees were required to register with the police. Amazingly, at the same time a German newspaper began offering tours through devastated Belgium.

Entertainment was held at the Temperance Hall when the refugees were joined by residents and committee members. A great deal of care had been taken to decorate the hall and provide a substantial meal for everyone. Musical entertainment was provided including the rendering of the Belgian National Hymn.

By mid 1915 the Registrar General estimated the number of Belgian refugees in the country to be 180,000, 65,000 men, 69,000 women and 46,000 children under 16. Plus 18,000 wounded and convalescent soldiers. By October 1915 30 refugees remained in Frome. A year later in October 1916 there were still in the region of 30 refugees who were all self-supporting, except for four young girls at the convent for whom clothing had to be supplied.

Reports in the *Somerset Standard* became fewer and fewer as the years rolled on, presumably indicating the integration of the refugees with the general population. They were no longer a novelty but a part of the fabric of the town. At least one of them played in the Frome Town Band.

As the war drew to a close it was reported in July 1918 that the Marchioness of Bath had been awarded the Insignia of the Medaille de la Reine Elisabeth in recognition of all of her work connected to the Belgian refugees.

The following is taken verbatim from the Somerset Standard of 14 March 1919

The Exodus of the Refugees

A memorable scene and one that will live long in the minds of those who witnessed it, took place at Frome station on Monday last week, [3rd March 1919] when a few of our townsmen assembled to say farewell to a party of 30 Belgian refugees who were leaving in a special carriage for Tilbury Docks *en route* to Antwerp. No words can describe the different appearance of these now happy people to the poor and terrified creatures, with haggard eyes and frightened look, who arrived in September 1914, fresh from the scene of the wrecking and burning of their homes, the slaughter of men, women and innocent children by cruel German soldiers, and the many other horrors of this awful war. For here in this land of peace and goodwill they had been well taken care of and made to feel wanted and not strangers. Many mutual friendships had sprung up so it was with mingled feelings of joy and sorrow that we bid them God-speed on their homeward journey. The writer of the above thinks it may at this juncture be interesting to relate just how these refugees came to Frome, and something about the work that the committee was called upon to do. He particularly wishes to refrain from mentioning any names on this committee, but there is one that stands out so prominently that, even at the risk of incurring his displeasure, he feels that it is only right to say how much the committee appreciated the unfailing devotion and ceaseless solicitude which Mr F White so continually showed for these poor people. He was the leading spirit in the movement from its very start and not for one moment did his interest ever flag.

Very soon after the outbreak of war, Mr White, realising the dire need of providing homes for the refugees, called a meeting of his townsmen at Mr Wheeler's auction mart. The gathering was enthusiastic and well attended and resulted in enough homes being promised to accommodate 60 refugees. In addition to these homes, two or three empty houses were placed at the disposal of the committee free of rent, furniture afterwards being borrowed and additions made to render them bright and cheerful. In one house, for instance, a mother and her seven children were accommodated, remaining there until their departure on Monday last week.

It was also considered necessary to start a special fund, it being felt that many would arrive absolutely destitute, and would require to be clothed etc; which fact afterwards proved to be only too true. A band of ladies undertook this task and canvassed the town with excellent results. Many in Frome also gave weekly sums, continuing this until the need for so doing ceased. Altogether quite £500 was raised in these two ways, every penny of which was spent carefully and advisedly. Meetings of the committee were held at frequent intervals and from time to time invitations were sent to London for more refugees. It would be difficult to say how many had been received in Frome, but the number is a large one, approximately 150, which speaks volumes for the hospitality of the town.

As the refugees gradually found employment less financial help was meted out to them, so that for some time prior to their departure no assistance had been necessary. This was an eminently satisfactory feature and one which did immense credit to Mr White and the committee.

In conclusion, we in Frome felt and still feel deeply grateful to the Belgian people for the miraculous and heroic way in which they held back the Germans during the first few critical weeks of the war. They probably at that time saved Europe from the slavery which our enemies would wish to have imposed upon us. By doing what we have for our refugees, we have in a practical way expressed our gratitude to a nation which has suffered more than any other, and which we now hope is on the threshold of a new era of happiness and prosperity.

[In May 1920 Mr F White, ex postmaster of Frome, and instigator of the committee to help the Belgian refugees, was honoured by the King of the Belgians – He was awarded the Palmes en argent l'Ordre de la Couronne – Silver palms of the order of the crown. He was given permission by the Foreign Office to wear the decoration in public in this country].

Unfortunately for those returning home it wasn't necessarily a case of happiness and prosperity. Some had difficulty in finding their homes after the desecration meted out by the Germans and found it hard to re-establish their previous lives. There was also some bad feeling amongst those who fled and those who stayed behind and experienced the occupation. As a result 100s returned to the UK in the 1920s

Little is known about the history of these people who were taken in throughout the UK, their experiences or that of their hosts. If you know of a family who took in the refugees or are related to one of those billeted in Frome or have anything to add to their story please get in touch via, publications@fsls.org.uk.

References

I have availed myself liberally of the *Somerset Standard* during 1913 – 1919, via the British Newspaper Archive. The photographs have been supplied to me by Alan F Taylor of the Folkestone & District Local History Society, to whom I am indebted. A history of Frome's part in the war is contained in *Frome in the Great War* by David Lassman.

FROME, WESSEX AND THE MAKING OF A NATION

Annette Burkitt

The pre-conquest period in England is a largely unknown and misunderstood period for the general reader. It hardly figures in educational settings below the undergraduate level. It is associated with generalised themes of horned helmets, blood and gore; its kings have unpronounceable names and unknown characters. Can a novelist put this right? It takes significant research and an academic approach to unlock the surprisingly large amount of surviving information to reach the treasure trove that is Anglo-Saxon history. Hard work, and then one is always open to criticism from purists. The ungovernable area of the imagination in a work of historical fiction is, perhaps, and understandably, unpalatable. Nevertheless, I have tried to peer through the gloom with speculative eyes to make something of a story, the story of early England, in which Wessex and Frome figure. Kings came to Frome throughout the Saxon period. They had a palace here, probably in the area which is known today as Saxonvale. They hunted in Selwood, feasted in the palace, went to church in the monastery church of St John and even died here, perhaps in a monastery hospital. Frome was a favourite place.

Mercia and Wessex became the dominant later kingdoms of the established Saxons. Their political interplay shaped the development of the nation. By the mid-tenth century Wessex kings were calling themselves kings of all Britain. How did this come about? And what became of the British inhabitants of Dumnonia, the kingdom of the 'Celtic' south-west? Looking in detail at the local landscape can help to answer this puzzle of hidden history.

Our understanding of the early years of the development of England suffers from the survival of few contemporary documentary sources, but settlement and events can be recognised and surmised through the archaeological record and from some well-known writings, notably by Gildas (sixth century), Bede (eighth century) and Nennius (ninth century). The Anglo-Saxon Chronicle and the Welsh Annals provide a framework for these and later years. A synthesis of research involving, in addition to original and secondary sources and archaeology, landscape studies, folklore, beliefs and place-names can give meat on the bones of this otherwise poorly recorded period of English history. Thankfully, later medieval writers, such as William of Malmesbury (twelfth century) were able to refer to or make copies of records of earlier times, which have fed the modern historian's understanding.

By the tenth century, Wessex, the last surviving Saxon kingdom after the Viking assaults of the late ninth century, stood out as the pre-eminent Saxon kingdom, with Winchester in Hampshire as its capital. The ancestor of King Alfred, Ecgberht, set the stage in the ninth century for the rise of the Wessex dynasty. By Athelstan's reign in the second quarter of the tenth century, Alfred's bloodline and his vision of a united England had become a reality. Wessex stretched across the whole of the south of Britain. Mercia, in the midlands, acquiesced to its dominance, somewhat unwillingly. Northumbria fluctuated in its loyalty to Wessex, disturbed by insurrection from the Scots, Irish Norse and Cumbrians. The mid tenth century inheritors of Alfred's vision, Edmund, Eadred, Eadwig and Edgar enjoyed the fruit of the earlier battles against Wessex's enemies by Edward, Alfred's son and his grandson Athelstan. They gathered troops, held witans (parliaments), hunted and practised diplomacy at star-studded palaces throughout southern England, travelling from palace to palace, requiring the presence of archbishops, bishops and ministers, as well as their individual retinues.

Saxon carvings embedded in the wall of St. John's church Frome. (Pilgrimage Trust)

The English were known on the continent for their rich apparel, their willingness to entertain foreigner diplomatic or learned, their ordered and well controlled civic life, their system of justice and particular their wealth, in treasure as well as enviable relics. The Church was well connected with the most notab monasteries in Europe and encouraged by popes and kings in its bold attempts to sustain a balance betwee civic and religious life, to the benefit of all. Naturally, the royal family of Wessex had close involveme with its chief protagonists, Dunstan, Aethelwold and Oswald.

Frome was one of the many palaces to which the Wessex kings travelled, from which a charter w published in December 934 AD. We know from this charter that King Athelstan attended a witan, in wh would have been a palace building in Frome, for the Christmas court. He had led a campaign in Scotla in the previous summer which attempted to unite all English and British kingdoms under his rule. He considered by many to be the first Saxon king to rule a united England.

The Frome area, now on the border between the counties of Somerset and Wiltshire, had been on t eastern frontier of Dumnonia with Wessex. The barrier forest of Selwood had assisted the British kingdc to remain independent for 200 years after the significant battle of Badon (c.517 AD), identified by sor as Bath, not far from Frome, which the British won. The Saxons, newly Christianised, swept westwards the late seventh century. The Celtic Christian British of Dumnonia were allowed to live on, as second-cla citizens, as shown by Alfred's laws.

After 720 AD, when Taunton in the west of Somerset was captured and the last Dumnonian king, Geraint, was killed (probably at Langport), the Britons gradually disappear from historical view, absorbed by inter-marriage, slavery or becoming peasantry. Their language, however, remains, fossilised, in some place-names, for instance in Bath (Bathon). The hilly landscape around Frome, dotted with prehistoric and later burials, forts and temples, retains traces of their long-established presence in place-names associated with pre-Christian belief systems and Christian saints. Somerset retains many town names associated with the post-Roman wave of Welsh Celtic Christian missionaries of the fifth and sixth centuries, for instance Lantocai, in Street near Glastonbury, Lan referring to the church of a Welsh saint.

Coin of King Athelstan died 939

In 934 AD Frome was already a place of significance in Wessex. As a religious missionary centre with a church (St John's) and monastery, it had been established more than two centuries before by Aldhelm, a close contact of King Ine. In addition to Athelstan's visit, King Eadred died in Frome in 955 AD, probably being nursed for his long-standing stomach ailment by monks. The palace and monastery buildings are long gone and the only trace of Saxon archaeology to be seen in Frome today is two stone cross shaft sculptures which have been incorporated into an inner wall of the restored parish church. The town was, with Amesbury and Cheddar, one of the favourite places of Athelstan, who relished hunting. The forest of Selwood would have been ideal for his needs. In 934 AD, 15 bishops, as well as both Archbishops, the kings Athelstan and Hywel Dda (the Good) of Wales, plus 25 ministers stayed here. By the early eleventh century Frome was important enough to have its own mint and was still owned by the Saxon kings at Domesday in 1086, but by then the monastery was no longer in existence, perhaps destroyed in the early eleventh century by the invasion of Sweyn Forkbeard and his son, Canute, who were active in south-central England.

The physical layout of the land and the doings of kings and bishops can be seen, but what about women and ordinary people and their thoughts?

The bare skeleton of the Anglo-Saxon Chronicle, together with the hagiographies, contemporary accounts and accounts by later historians give a flavour of the early medieval period in England, especially of the delicate balancing act of Church and State. During the tenth century, a massive religious movement, a reformation, was underway. This was a successful, organised attempt to enforce the stricter forms of Roman Catholicism, led by powerful bishops, notably Dunstan and Aethelwold, a process which was brought to an end in the sixteenth century by Henry VIII and his chief minister, Thomas Cromwell. How and why the growing tenth century mindset of pilgrimage, relics, miracles, saints and their related monetary indulgences, along with the concept of Purgatory, came to be preeminent in the lives of all social strata of the tenth and later centuries are fruitful areas for the interested novelist. We can follow the birth of the Benedictine reform movement in the lives of Saint Dunstan and Aethelwold, who determinedly navigated their way, at many times thwarted by kings, through many years and many reigns. They both enjoyed long, active lives. They were often assisted by the women of the Wessex court, particularly Eadgifu, the wife of Edward, mother to kings Eadmund and Eadred and grandmother to two more kings, Eadwig and Edgar.

Edward the Martyr and Aethelred complete the long-lived dynasty of Alfred and bring the domination of Wessex to a close. The bloodline goes on to Edward the Confessor, but England by the mid eleventh century is no longer the force that it was.

Historians and writers may guess at the struggles of power between the tough-minded church leaders and their equally hard-nosed secular rivals in the Wessex dynasty. As in any age, jealousy, espionage, murder, bigotry, bribery, greed and a contradictory wish to be seen to be altruistic and to save one's soul must have been rampant then, as now. A deeply-held belief by society in the efficacy of relics to maintain health, win wars and quell devils, threads through the imaginative mind of the age like the serpents on stone cross-shafts. Thegns, freemen and slaves would all have been subject to the delights and terrors of the tenth century vision of Heaven and Hell.

The palaces of the Saxon kings are long gone, like the homes and habitations of the Britons before them. The early English kings hardly figure in history books. Their names are forgotten, too difficult to say, their achievements unheeded. The Church, through its two reformations, won the battle for longevity. The everyday struggle for power and dominance, the survival of the fittest, peeps through in the landscape and historical record.

Annette's novels *Flesh and Bones of Frome Selwood and Wessex*, and its sequel *The Gorge* are published by Hobnob Press and available from Frome Museum & Winstone's Hunting Raven bookshop.

Frome Harvest 1910

A POP-UP FOSSIL MUSEUM IN FROME

Breathing new life into an old geological collection

Simon Carpenter

Between the start of the New Year and the Coronavirus outbreak, the writer created a weekly Pop-up Fossil Museum in Frome to help raise funds for Somerset Earth Science Centre. The fossils had come from an old collection formerly belonging to Stonar School near Bath and were mostly collected by Philip Werran Curnow a former teacher of archaeology and geology at that school. As well as selling fossils, the pop-up museum provided an opportunity to engage and educate the public about the local geology and to promote the work of Somerset Earth Science Centre. This article sets out some of the background to this initiative.

In October 2019, the writer became custodian of the Stonar School Geological Collection which included a substantial number of minerals and fossils collected by the late Philip Werran Curnow (1912 –1992), a former teacher of archaeology and geology at Stonar near Bath. In the summer of 2004, the school geology department closed. The geology collections associated with it were no longer required and were eventually stored in a barn. It seems that the collections remained in this poor environment for some considerable time before the writer collected them in October 2019.

Many people had given rock, fossil and mineral specimens to the school geological collection including Elizabeth Devon, former head of geology at the school and chair of the Bath Geological Society, the late John & Pat Bevan-Jones, the late George Hibberd, Charles Hiscock, the late Ron Smith, Christopher Steane, the late Pat Bennett and Malcolm Tucker. Geology students at the school and members of Bath Geological Society also added to the collection, but the biggest contribution came from Philip Curnow. The Stonar Collection suffered from lack of associated documentation, something that is difficult to correct or improve retrospectively. Because of the lack of information and limited research potential, most of the collection was destined to be used in 'handling' collections.

Philip Werran Curnow

Philip Curnow whose private collection was donated to the school following his death in the summer of 1992, had taught archaeology and geology at the school. There are no field note books associated with Philip's collection and we know precious little about his interests and activities other than his passion for Cornish geology (Elizabeth Devon, personal communication). His wife, Margaret Curnow, was deputy headmistress of Stonar School until her death in July 1990. Philip was elected a Fellow of the Geological Society of London on 21 June 1950 (no.7039) but was removed from the list at the council meeting of 8 January 1964 – although no specific reason is given (Richard Ashley and Caroline Lam, Geological Society of London, personal communication). On Philip Curnow's admission form to become a Fellow of the Society, his student profession is crossed out and followed by, 'As from Aug 1st – Curator of Geology, Bristol City Museum'. At this time, Philip's address was, 31 Sciennes Road, Edinburgh EH9. He had just completed an honours degree course in geology at Edinburgh University, with his final examination in July 1950. With a new role beckoning at Bristol City Museum, it is likely he moved from Scotland shortly after becoming a Fellow to take up his new post in Bristol.

Philip's Collection contains both minerals and fossils. The dates on specimen labels suggest that his most active period of collecting occurred during the 1960s. Back then, access to quarries to collect fossils and minerals was less problematic than it is today; there was certainly less concern over health & safety. Many of Philip's geological specimens from the Mendip Hills in Somerset, for example, come from Carboniferous limestone quarries where access today is almost completely forbidden on safety grounds. The fossils in the Curnow Collection are almost exclusively invertebrates and include some interesting and diverse material including well-preserved Silurian, Carboniferous and Jurassic corals. Local fossils are represented by ammonites, bivalves, gastropods, brachiopods, sponges and plants. There are a small number of vertebrate fossils including some shark teeth from the Blackheath member of Abbey Wood, London and some fragments of Late Triassic bone bed conglomerate from the Westbury Formation of Aust, South Gloucestershire. The collection has been obtained mostly from UK fossiliferous localities, but there are also a few exotic/foreign specimens in the collection.

Much of the collection is without identifying numbers or codes. The written information in each specimen tray is also limited. For example, a fossil coral specimen in the Curnow collection may simply say 'Jurassic' and 'Bath area'. Scientific names are used when known, but regrettably, detailed stratigraphy, a desirable requirement for most research collections, is missing.

The Stonar School Collection has a few rare and interesting fossil specimens including the crab, *Plagiophthalmus oviformis* Bell from the Wilmington Sand Member of Wilmington Quarry, Devon, collected by Curnow and an 'ex-Stonar School' specimen. This fossil was donated to the Natural History Museum, London on Saturday 2 November 2019 by Simon Carpenter. A small collection of sponge fossils from the Faringdon Sponge Formation have also been identified and given as a donation to Oxford Museum where they will be used to make up a small handling collection in Philip's name for use in their schools outreach. A small number of fossil graptolites have also been donated to Bristol City Museum.

The bulk of the Stonar School Collection will be offered as handling material to Somerset Earth Science Centre, in particular the mineral collection. The centre, based at Moons Hill Quarry, Stoke St Michael, works closely with schools, colleges, universities and community groups across Somerset to improve their understanding of the natural world and the earth sciences in particular. Although some fossils are destined for the centre, a large number of small invertebrate fossils were retained to offer for sale in Frome as part of an exciting new pop up fossil museum initiative.

A Pop-Up Fossil Museum in Frome

In January 2020, the first Pop-up Fossil Museum was set up as part of the Wednesday Flea Market at the Cheese & Grain, Frome. The writer and his volunteer helpers were keen to engage the public, not just to sell the fossils but to explain what they are and how they help us understand the evolution of the Earth. The writer, intending to make the whole project as sustainable as possible, cycled all the fossils and props to the market venue each week

| Volunteer Helen Deeming (L), at the Cheese & Grain. | Rose Heaword, a volunteer helping to pack up the bicycle with the fossils |

The fossils were generally sold for nominal amounts, but even so, over a period of about three months, until Coronavirus put a stop to it, over £350 was raised for the Earth Science Centre which will be able to use some of these funds to display the more showy fossils and minerals. During the school half-term week, staff from the Centre came to the market to help with the stall on what was to be our busiest day. Kids do like fossils! The public were encouraged to bring in their own fossils for identification and as a consequence, the writer became acquainted with a number of local collectors, all with fascinating collections.

Labels were attached to the sold fossils to identify them, their age and provenance including a reference to Stonar School. As the collection becomes more widely dispersed, this reference will help perpetuate the legacy of the collection as well the collector, Philip Curnow. Had the collection not been rescued when it was, it may well have been discarded altogether and an opportunity to use it to inspire and interest would have been lost forever.

Thanks

I would like to start by offering my sincere gratitude to Stonar School for relinquishing care of their geological collection so it can be refreshed and used with the geological community elsewhere. Elizabeth Devon, former Head of Geology at the school alerted me to the threats facing the school geology collection and has helped provide information about the collection and collectors. I am indebted to Richard Ashley for finding out more about Philip Werran Curnow. I would also like to thank Alan Bentley, friend and geologist for helpful comments and discussions during the course of this project and for assisting in the identification of the fossils and minerals. The running of the pop-up was only possible with the kind volunteer support of Rose Heaword, Helen Deeming, William Mitchell, Steve Smith and the team from Somerset Earth Science Centre. Finally, I would like to thank the many people who gave their rocks, fossils and minerals to Stonar School and in particular, the contribution made by Philip Curnow.

A HOUSE WARMING AT FROME 1786

From: *Retrospections of the Stage*. John Bernard,[1] 1830.

Transcribed by ALM

Handy,[2] a tavern-keeper at Bath, was about to open the principal inn (The George) at Frome, which being the property of Lord Cork, various members of the 'Catch Club'[3] were invited to the house-warming. Captains Baker and Stanley, Sir Charles Bampfylde, Incledon[4] and myself, went over in a party.

The friends and tenants from his Lordship's estate amounted to about forty, and the visitors from Bath to as many more; the dinner tickets were half-a-guinea, exclusive of liquors. When we were all assembled in the parlours and before the door, shaking hands, and deciding bets upon the time of each other's arrival, Captain Stanley's head, running upon an object more important, led him to enter the bar and ascertain the quality of the wines to be imbibed. Mrs Handy drew the cork of a Madeira bottle, and filled him a glass. The epicure took it into his mouth and rolled it deliberately about the tip of his tongue, but shook his head, and remarked, "That won't do, Mrs Handy - that won't do; 'tis as weak as tea!"

Mrs Handy expressed her regret, said she would speak to her husband the instant he came in, and some other should be substituted. The Captain then returned to the company.

I now took an opportunity of going to the bar to shake the worthy host's hand, who directly after made his appearance, and was informed by his wife of the Captain's objection. Handy smiled and gave me a glass from the bottle, which I thought was very good. He then drew a glass of brandy, poured it into the undervalued liquid, and corked it up. The Captain soon returned, his peace of mind being essentially disturbed by the prospect of poor Madeira. Handy instantly apologized for (what he termed) his wife's mistake in giving a sample from a bottle not designed for the dinner, and begged the Captain's opinion upon another. Producing and filling a glass from the same, the Captain subjected it to his former ordeal, bathing his tongue in it, and scouring the roof of his mouth; an immediate effect was perceptible in his countenance, which glooming the instant before like the dead of night, lit up with a spreading smile like the dawn of a red sky in a dog-day morning. Concluding the ceremony with a smack sharp and loud as the pop of champagne, he exclaimed, "Ah, that's something like, Handy; there's some strength in that - that's what I call a glass of good Madeira."

About nine o'clock Lord Cork vacated the chair, and I was called to it. The country-people were so astonished at our pleasantry and music, that they began to get exhilarated at an early hour; but, as this was overthrowing an established habit of the Club, I proposed that we should adjourn to the theatre, and return to our glasses about eleven. This was agreed by about two-thirds of the party, and we consequently pretty well filled the front-boxes. The entertainment was the *West Indian*,[5] in which Dowton[6] played Belcour, then a young member of the profession, but with more than the usual evidences of future eminence.

Incledon, recognizing some acquaintance in the company, went behind the scenes, and directly after volunteered a song; this was a high treat to the pit and gallery; but the wags in the boxes were bent on other amusement. They encored him twice, and brought him on the stage for the fourth time. He now perceived their intention, and, making a low bow, addressed them as follows: - "Gentlemen, I sang this song, for the first time, to please my friends behind the scenes; the second, to please the public; the third, to please yourselves; but if I sing it again, may I be *********!" (stopping as if to meditate a terrific oath.) "What?" shouted a dozen voices. "Why, I'll whisper you, Gentlemen, when I come round;" and with these words he returned to the boxes. This was the cleverest thing I ever knew Incledon to say or do."

The George, extreme right, in about 1865 the earliest known photograph.

Footnotes

[1] JOHN BERNARD 1756 - 1828
Born Southampton 1756, His father, a Lt in the navy, placed him in a solicitors office in the hope that he would check his desire to go on the stage. Bernard ran away to Bristol, at 17, where he enquired into the nature of theatricals in the vicinity and was told that a Mr Thornton, who governed a band of 'dramatic desperados' at the village of Chew Magna, was the nearest manager; a fellow lodger who belonged to a 'Spouting Club' told Bernard that Thornton was looking for recruits. Bernard and the other lodger studied a scene from 'Venice Preserv'd' and delivered the piece. Thornton was favourably impressed and offered to let Bernard try his abilities on his boards the following week.
In May 1773 Bernard made his public debut in Chew Magna in the character of Jaffier (one of the principal characters in Otway's 'Venice Preserv'd').
The theatre was fitted up in the interior of a malthouse. According to Bernard there was a 'reasonable wardrobe and one or two scenes not so old as himself.' The first night's receipts amounted to £9; a second performance was given and Bernard's name inserted in the playbills as 'Mr Budd - a young gentleman of only 17 years of age in his first appearance on any stage.' After the second night's performance Thornton gave Bernard his share of the receipts viz 8/- and three tallow candles of Bristol manufacture. The season at Chew Magna lasted four weeks.
He made his London debut in 1787 in 'The Beaux Stratagem' and left for America in 1797. His first appearance there was in New York the same year. He remained in America for 20 years as actor manager at various theatres. He married three times and died in poverty in 1828 in London. The 'Retrospections' were published in two vols in 1830 and in 1850 a further selection was published.
[2] Thomas Handy was landlord at the George Inn from 1786 - 1791
[3] This club was got up by Sir John Danvers and John Bernard in 1784. It was envisaged there would be about 50-100 members with a guinea subscription and meetings would take place weekly. Sir John Danvers donated £10 at the outset. The club would embrace all the musical talent both amateur and professional in the city and neighbourhood. The committee comprised:
Sir John Danvers, Earl Conyingham (Chairman), Lord Cork, Sir Charles Bampfylde, Sir Charles Asgill, Captain Baker, Captain Tucker, Dr Harrington (Composer & Physician), Sgnr. Rauzzini (Musical Conductor 1747-1810 b. Rome. He arrived in Bath c1777 where he remained for the rest of his life. Tenor, Teacher and Conductor. He composed operas and other music. Friend of Mozart. Buried in Bath Abbey); Loder, Meyler (Poet Laureate) and Bernard. A room at the White Lion was booked where the host was Arnold.
Forty persons subscribed in the first fortnight with which they bought music and instruments. After a month 100 members had been enrolled.
Fines:
Oaths   1/-
Politics 2/-
Religion 3/-
Quarrel or dispute - a dozen of claret.
Members were allowed to bring friends. A certain number of pieces to be sung at each meeting with 5-10-minute intervals for conversation.
[4] CHARLES INCLEDON 1763-1826
Singer and actor, a pupil of Rauzzini. Sometimes known as The Cornish Tenor or The Prince of Ballad Singers. He was the principal English tenor of his day and sang in both opera and oratorio, but was most popular singing ballads.
[5] A play by Richard Cumberland. First performed Drury Lane 1771.
[6] WILLIAM DOWTON 1764-1851 actor. Began training as an architect but ran away from home and joined a company of strolling players. First performance on a stage at Ashburton 1781. Appeared in many leading roles at Drury Lane and the Haymarket.

§§§§

THE MASS LABOUR DEMONSTRATION OF 1917

Taken from the *Somerset Standard* 21 September 1917

The demonstration at Portway

People flocked in their hundreds to Wallbridge and later to Broadway on Sunday afternoon to take part in, or to witness, the first great labour demonstration held in Frome. Frome Town Military Band headed a procession of members of the Workers' Union and the National Union of Railwaymen and kindred organisations who were marshalled by the officers of the local Trades and Labour Council. This body had been recently formed to coordinate the various unions and members of those who are not strong enough to constitute branches. Two of them are particularly strong, the Railwaymen's and the Workers' Unions, the latter having very rapidly developed, stimulated, no doubt, by some concessions of employers for the advantage of their work people. The council have adopted an ambitious or, - as they declared on the authority of the Premier, an audacious programme. They contemplate not merely combined action for the increase of wages and betterment of the condition of the workers, but also direct representation on public bodies and influence in local affairs generally.

Three of the principal officials of the Trades and Labour Council headed the procession, walking in front of the band. Two large silk banners were borne one being that of the Workers' Union and the other that of the Bath branch of the Railwaymen's Union. Half a dozen females followed the first banner, then between 150 and 200 men - the actual numbers varied from point to point - 60 to 70 more women and girls, and nearly a couple of hundred men succeeded the second banner. The route taken was by Locks Hill, Keyford, Christchurch Street, Badcox, Nunney Road, and Portland Road to the Cooperative Society's field at Broadway. Here an

79

open-air meeting was held around a lorry which served as a platform for the speakers. The number present was between 2000 and 3000 of all classes, women workers and others not employed for wages, being in full force. Mr E Hill presided, supported by Messer's G. Brown, National Union of Railwaymen, Matt Giles, Bristol Organiser for the West of England of the Workers' Union, J Ramsden, Birmingham, of the Brass Workers' Unions, Mrs Hayes of a London Printers Association and local officers of the organisations named and the Trades and Labour Council. The banners were displayed behind the lorry.

The demonstration passes The Ship Inn Christchurch Street

The chairman said that the day celebrated the fulfilment of a dream some of them had had in the past - the formation of a trades and Labour Council in Frome. There were represented on the council seven organisations with a membership of over 1000. That had been brought about by the advent of the workers' union and the loyal cooperation of the Railwaymen's Union. They were looking forward to the future with great hopes for the working classes. As chairman of that council he wished to say a few words as to the line they propose to take. They were *bona fide* a Trades and Labour Council. They allowed no other sections of the community to use them as a stalking horse, but if any member of a branch of a trades union wished to join them, he would be welcomed. They had made the constitution of the Council as democratic as possible. They would welcome all trades unionists no matter how small the branch, who were prepared to work shoulder to shoulder with them for the purpose of achieving something for the good of the working classes in Frome.

They had a resolution which would be put before that meeting as to the formation of the Local Food Committee. They submitted to the Urban Council six names of members as possible candidates. He criticised the way in which the submission had been met, and the failures to

80

find qualities referred to in the committee. They, as representing a thousand consumers wished to take their share in carrying on local government in Frome. It was ill mannered to cast a slur upon an organisation which had only been in existence a few weeks to say they had not done their share in the government of Frome in the past and that therefore they ought not to have the honour conferred upon it of being allowed to serve now. They intended to serve in the future.

They had selected candidates for the various municipal bodies for the Urban Council and for the Guardians who would come forward after ratification by the Labour Council. This was in view of any vacancy that might occur. They could therefore claim that they were prepared to take their share in the local government of Frome. They were determined to get fair and adequate representation on all local bodies and they were fully confident that by united efforts and support of the bodies constituting the council they would carry four of the seats at least in the next Council election in Frome, (applause). They had made up their minds that labour should be directly represented, and would pursue their course undisturbed by any criticism from outside. The resolution which had been drafted to be submitted to them was as follows:-

> That this mass meeting of organised labour in Frome and district welcomes the formation of the Trades and Labour Council, and hereby pledges itself to work for the complete organisation of all workers, industrially and politically, believing that by these means only will the workers bring about their emancipation; and further enters its emphatic protest against the constitution of the local Food Committee believing its present constitution to be a violation of the fundamental principles, viz, the safeguarding of the interest of the consumers and pledges itself to use every means in its power to secure on this and all other local bodies direct an adequate Labour representation.

The resolution was proposed by Mr CH. Angel of the National Union of Railwaymen in a vigorous speech. He reminded them that Lloyd George had told them to be audacious. The policy of labour would have to be that those who worked would live, but those who did not work --. He claimed that as working classes they were entitled to 50% representation on local bodies.

Mr Curtis, chairman of the Frome branch of the Workers' Union seconded the resolution, and said that the workers had made up their minds that the time had come to manage their own affairs, and not to let others do it for them. They had long needed direct representation to watch the interests of the working classes.

The motion was put to the meeting and carried unanimously.

They had concluded that wages in Frome were not comparable with those in other places. They had a return which showed where the maximum wage in Frome for a labourer was 18 shillings per week, many were only getting 14 to 16 shillings a week. They could, in this country, as the war had proved, produce anything that was needed. Three millions of their strongest men had been withdrawn from productive labour and sent to work of destruction. On the war and the equipment and necessities of war they had been spending £5,000,000 to £6,000,000 and now getting on for £7,000,000 a day. Before the war if anybody had said that they could spend that amount they would have been considered fit only for a lunatic asylum. It was pointed out how vast an amount of advantage to the working classes could be in future obtained for much smaller expenditure. The working classes would demand greater leisure comfort and culture given to them that their children should have better opportunities than they had had. They had come to the trades unions because they were discontented with the conditions under which they had to work. They had been unorganised and therefore could not improve them.

In Frome there were over 1000 directly represented on the Trades and Labour Council and he pointed out the power possessed by such a body of people in any united effort. The amount of food stuffs which could be obtained for £1in July 1914 now cost £2.10 shillings to £2.15 shillings and even if wages went up 75% beyond the pre-war rates it did not meet the extra cost of living.

It was announced that 150 employees of Messer's Butler & Tanner had now joined the union. Mrs Hayes of the London Printers Union said that she had worked for 25 years in the printing trade and Frome had always been looked upon as one of the worst and blackest spots in that trade.

A motion of thanks was passed to the speakers and the proceedings terminated.

Co-op Fields Broadway

FROME PORTRAITS 25

REV JOHN SKINNER 1772-1839

Oil painting of John Skinner in Radstock Museum

John Skinner was the rector of the parish of Camerton for 39 years from 1800 until he blew his brains out in a nearby wood in 1839. His occupation was one to which he was particularly unsuited. He and his parishioners disliked each other intently. High minded, scholarly, quick to judge and short tempered he had little time for his flock of drunken, brawling, fornicating miners.

He developed a passion for the emerging science of archaeology and the study of prehistory. In conjunction with one of his few friends, Sir Richard Colt-Hoare of Stourhead, he embarked upon a programme of excavating and recording the many prehistoric remains which occurred in his locality. Between them they opened many dozens of barrows which they sketched and recorded according to the custom of the time, seeking to understand who had built them and why rather than collecting artefacts. His activities produced over 100 large journals full of illustrations now in the British Library largely unexamined and unpublished. With failing health, few friends, his family largely deceased and the pressure of his parishioners he took his own life at the age of 67.

BEGGARS BUSH

Neil Howlett

Beggars Bush was a common place name in many counties of England, Wales and Scotland. The earliest record I have found dates to 1528, but most are between 1600 and 1750. It then declined, and in many places the name is no longer used. This article explores what is known of the sites in and around Frome. It will also explore the origin of the name and how it came to have a wide distribution based on an analysis of 120 sites where the place name Beggars Bush has been recorded, and examples of use in literature. I have posted evidence, references and detailed analysis at www.beggarsbush.org.uk. I have been helped by too many generous people to name them all here. Further additions and corrections are welcome. The explanation for the name given in many anthologies is that these were places where beggars congregated. That is what the Oxford English Dictionary will tell you. The OED is wrong. The prosaic but better explanation is that it is a derogatory name for poor land. The local sites in and around Frome are consistent with this.

The editors of the English Place Name Society volume for Wiltshire describe it as 'uncomplimentary'.[1] John Field, discussing *Beggary*, noted the difficulty in separating the literal from the figurative use of beggar.[2] In early modern England 'beggars' were not necessarily itinerants; they were called vagrants, vagabonds, rogues or Egyptians. Beggars could be labourers, or householders fallen on hard times. The beggars at 'Beggars Bushes' were the owners or occupiers of marginal land.

Sites in and around Frome

The 'Beggars Bushes' recorded in and around Frome form clusters, at Critchill (West Woodland Parish), Oldford, (Frome & Berkley parishes) Lullington, (Lullington, Lavington & Hemington parishes).

Critchill – West Woodlands

The earliest record is in the *Perambulation of West Woodlands*, (1605-1606).[3] This records the parish boundary between West Woodlands and Frome going up the Broadway towards Cottles Oak, turning at White Cross, 'along the Way that leadeth Southwards towards Marston and so along the said Way unto Beggars Bush and then along the Way South cross the way that goeth over to Tytherington'. White Cross must be the junction of Broadway with Portland Road, so this puts Beggars Bush along or off Portland Road, Dommetts Lane, Green Lane and Marston Lane. This was across the headland of the West Field. It is not possible to fix the location more precisely.

Leases granted by John Champneys of Lullington probably refer to the same location. A lease dated 29 Dec 1675 refers to one acre of arable land in the West Field, 'near Beggars Bushe . . . the east end shooting upon toward' Marston Lane.[4]A lease dated 1 Aug 1707 records, 'near Beggars Bush . . .the east shooting down toward' Marston Lane.[4]Another Champney's Lease dated 2 April 1679 refers to '4 acres of arable land in the South field of F*[rome]* S*[elwood]* to a bush there called Beggars Bush the publique way leading from F.S. to Marston Biggott on the east end, and another publique way leading from the West end of Frome to Critchill . . . on the south side'.[5]This is unusual in referring to an actual bush. There is also record in Town Tything recorded in the Land Tax assessment of 1766 as, 'ground late Beggars Bush'. It is not possible to fix the location. The name is not recorded in this area in the Tithe Apportionment of 1840 or the Cruse Survey of 1813.

Oldford Hill

Oldford - Frome Parish

An Indenture dated 10th September 1635 of church lands leased to Richard Treasure, includes

> '. . . *and* also other three acres of the said ten acres doe lye in another field of Frome Selwood aforesaid called the Northfeild that is to say one acre of the said three acres doth lye nere Beggers bushe the way leading to Bartley [Berkley] on the Northside thereof and the land of S[r] Thomas Thynne knight in the tenure of William Johnsons on the Southside thereof .. [6]

A Deed of 28 and 29 August 1750 defines land as 'abutting on the south to the highway leading from Beggar's Bush (or Oldford-hill) to Berkley'.[7]

The survey by Jeremiah Cruse (1813) records seven fields named 'At Beggar's Bush', and shows a larger area with 'Beggars Bush' written across it parallel to the road from Fromefield at the top Oldford Hill. This was once occupied by the Mendip Lodge Hotel. Again, this is exposed land across the top of the escarpment.

Fig 1

Cruse Map of Oldford with Beggars Bush fields outlined.
The fields numbered 1087 are in Berkley

Chart 1 – Extracts from the Cruse Survey 1814 [8]

No.	Premises	State	A	R	P	Proprietor	Tenure	Tenant
553	At Beggars Bush	Mea.	2	1	8	Wayland & Muir	on lives	Thomas Paines Wo.
554	Philip's Paddock at Do.	Past.	0	2	20	Sarah Miller	B lives	William Dainty
555	Paddock at Beggars Bush	Ara.	0	1	19	George Kingdom	in fee	Joseph Jesser
556	At Beggars Bush ~~Further ground at Cuckow Hill~~ crossed out	Ara.	4	3	3	Edward Barnard's Execs	Lives	William Baily
557	Do.	Mea.	1	0	3	Wayland & Muir	on lives	Thomas Paines Wo.
558	Do.	Do.	1	0	33	Do.	Do.	Do.
580	Long Ground near Beggars Bush	Mea.	2	1	18	James Ayres	In fee	William Baily

The 1840 Tithe Apportionment records four fields named 'At Beggars Bush'. It is difficult to cross-relate the fields between Cruse and the Tithe Survey. The Tithe Apportionment map is damaged at the fold line which runs through the sites, so none of them is specifically identifiable on the map. However, they are in the same area as the fields on the Cruse Survey.

Chart 2 Extracts from the Frome Tithe Apportionment 1840

No.	Premises	Type	A	R	P	Owner	Occupier	£ s d
888	At Beggars Bush	Pasture	2	1	17	Elizabeth Olive	Benjamin King	18/-/-
890	At Beggars Bush	Arable	5	32	7	Elizabeth Olive	Enoch Ham	18/-/-
891	At Beggars Bush	Pasture	1	-	3	Elizabeth Olive	Benjamin King	1/6
892	At Beggars Bush	Pasture	1		34	Elizabeth Olive	Benjamin King	7/1

All these names are 'At Beggars Bush' which suggest the Beggars Bush itself was either the larger area, including what is now Frome College playing fields. linking to the Beggars Bush fields in Berkley, or possibly a more specific point location. The text across the Cruse map suggests it was an area, not a point.

Oldford - Berkley Parish

The Tithe Awards for Berkley (1839) also record the name for part of Berkley Parish which was south of Berkley Lane in the area of what is now Beaconsfield Farm behind the College playing fields. Although not contiguous the four of the fields in Frome were owned by

Elizabeth Olive who also held two of the fields in Berkley. That suggests the name may have been given or perpetuated by her.

Chart 3. Berkley Tithe Apportionment

No.	Premises	Type	A	R	P	Owner	Occupier
84a	Beggars Bush	Arable	2	2	14	Bath the Marques of	Robert Jefferys
84b	Beggars Bush	Arable	1	-	12	Mordaunt Sir John Baronet	Robert Jefferys
85	Beggars Bush	Arable	1	3	8	Elizabeth Olive	John Nicholls
86	Beggars Bush	Arable	1	1	29	Elizabeth Olive	John Nicholls

The land is at the top of a north facing escarpment, flat and open to the elements. There are two pieces of evidence which might support the theory that this was a site used by itinerant travellers, but I do not find either convincing. The road from the crossroads towards Berkley is now called Gypsy Lane, but it was called Berkley Lane until the late nineteenth century. Also, in June 1814 the Constable for Frome, Isaac Gregory, records in his diary evicting an encampment of 'gypsies' from Oldford Hill. However, Gregory did not call them *beggars* or the area *Beggars Bush*. The entry suggests they were camping further down the hill[9].

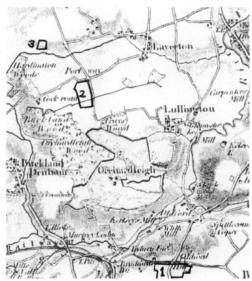

Fig. 2 Lullington, Laverton and Hemington Beggars Bushes. Parish boundaries in red. 1 Oldford, 2 Lullington & Laverton 3 Hemington, Lullington/Laverton& Hemington

The sites in Lullington, Laverton and Hemington are about two miles from Oldford as the crow flies, and until the 1620s there was a direct route through Orchardleigh, until that was blocked when the Champneys family emparked most of the parish.

The Lullington/Laverton fields are to left of the road from Lullington to Faulkland, just before the crossroads with Cock Road, which goes from Laverton village to Buckland Dinham. Like the Oldford site the fields form one site straddling the parish boundary, open and exposed, and again the name is now forgotten.

The earliest reference I have found is in 1807 and although this implied possible use as far back as 1722 the name is not mentioned in earlier records for the area.

The Hemington field is across the valley to the north, a couple of field off the same road, known here as Portway. It is a single exposed field. The fields in Hemington and Laverton were owned and occupied by the same family at the time of the Tithe Survey, who appeared to have occupied these and several adjoining fields since the 1770s.

The meaning of the name in Hemington is clear from the names of the adjacent fields recorded in the Tithe Survey. These are derogatory; 'Gutter Land, Poor or Little Mead Portway, Long Bush, and close by Poor Tyning, Little Poor Tyning, and Cuckoo's Nest'. Indeed, the parish of Hemington offers an almost complete range of derogatory field names, from the straightforward, (Biggs Poor Ground, Sinklands, Strong Mans, Dismal Down, Poor Ground, Little & Great Bramble Hill, Well Use and Cats Tails, Poor Fields, Sparrow Bills, Little Slough, and Great Slough), to the ironic, (Twerton Revel). In addition to the Beggars Bush are Irendell Bush, Briers Close, 6 Acre Bushy Ground, and Blackthorn Hedge.

Fig 3 Lullington Field Names

At Lullington/Laverton the adjacent field names near Beggars Bush are similar. They include Fox Holes, Folly, Kid's Feast, and Barren Close Hill (although Hunger Hill is likely to be from AS for wooded slope). There is also Coldharbour, a derogatory name which Richard Coates has demonstrated to be a proverbial usage derived from the notorious decayed mansion of that name in London.[10] Coldharbour and Beggars Bush appear close together in several places.

There is also historical evidence of the poor quality of this land. In 1794 the Surveyor William Simpson remarked that in Laverton the 'arable land . . is poor and stiff, requiring great strength to plow it, yielding but poor crops', with pernicious weeds so that sheep could not be grazed upon it for manure. On a map dated 1818 the Lullington 'Beggars Bush' is annotated with the word 'teasels'. A local farmer told me he knew it well as when he was a child before the Second World War as he had been paid to plant mangles there to improve the soil.

Beggars Bush – Literary use

Beggars Bush emerged from the large stock of proverbial phrases popular in early modern England. Servants were known by their livery and saints by their emblems. Beggars had their emblems --- staffs, bags, bowls and bushes. The symbolic nature of the association is shown by the existence of precursor phrases. In 1506 Isabel Plumpton wrote from Yorkshire to her husband in London urging him to end costly litigation there; 'Sir for God sake take an end, for we are brought to begger staffe'.

There is evidence for a clear and consistent usage of 'Beggars Bush' meaning to fall into poverty, sometimes by one's own folly. In *Her Protection for Women* (1589) the pseudonymous Jane Anger wrote;

> The great Patrimonies that wealthy men leave their children after their death, make them rich: but vice and other marthriftes happening into their companies, never leave them until they bee at the beggers bush, where I can assure you they become poore.

The broadside ballad *London's Ordinary* (1674-89) associated characters with inn names; it was the spendthrifts who went to the Beggars Bush. This was based on a song by Thomas Heywood (1608) in which the bankrupts go to the 'World's End'.

As Adam Fox has shown, the relationship between oral and written culture in early modern England was complex.[9] Fox argues that oral use is sufficient for the preservation, maintenance and communication of a word or phrase (see above Elizabeth Olive who owned several fields with that name in different parishes) but that literary use is required for distribution. I would add to that dramatic performance and maps.

A key source for distribution was *The Beggars Bush,* a play written by John Fletcher and Philip Massinger in 1622, but printed in the 'Beaumont and Fletcher' canon. Through print and performance this is likely to have made a substantial contribution to the survival and distribution of the literary phrase. For the next century 'Beaumont & Fletcher' plays were performed more often than Shakespeare's. When the ban on plays was lifted in 1660 *The Beggars Bush* was put on by three different companies in London. Pepys went to see it four times, including, 'the first time that ever I saw woman come upon the stage'. New versions and an opera were written, though after the Glorious Revolution scenes the scenes with stupid cowardly 'Boors' (Dutchmen) were removed. It was chosen in 1764 for the re-opening of the Theatre Royal Drury Lane before the King and Queen, and featured in Edmund Kean's acclaimed 'Shakespeare' season at Drury Lane in 1815 and 1816.

There are also many records of regional performances including at Bath and Salisbury. An extract *The Lame Common-Wealth*, containing canting exchanges from the play, was included in *The Wits, or Sport for Sport (1672)* a collection of 'drolls' advertised as:-

> fitted for the pleasure and content of all persons, either in court, city, country, or camp' and "presented and shewn for the merriment and delight of wise men, and the ignorant, as they have been sundry times acted in publique, and private, in London . . . in the countrey at . . . faires, in halls and taverns, on several mountebancks stages, . . ., by several stroleing players, fools, and fidlers, and the mountebancks zanies, with loud laughter, and great applause.

This included the crowning of the character Clause as King of the Beggars, and features canting phrases. The scene was borrowed by many other authors, and the character Clause took on a life of his own. The scene and Clause, presented as a real event, appeared in the many editions of *The Life and Adventures of Bampfylde Moore Carew; King of the Beggars* (1745) and *An Apology for the Life of Bampfylde Moore Carew* (1749), a separate work probably written by the Sherborne publisher Robert Goadby. As to the eponymous 'Beggars Bush' itself the play is vague. It is a meeting place for the beggar characters, led by Clause, who is not a beggar at all but a wrongfully deposed Earl. It is not a real place; the play is not set in England, but in and around Bruges.

E Cobham Brewer - mischief and maps

Beggars Bush was included in many collections of proverbs in this sense, but became confused with a real place. *Brewer's Dictionary of Phrase and Fable* (1868 until very recent editions) gave;

> 'Beggars Bush. To go by beggar's bush, or Go home by beggar's bush – i.e. to go to ruin. Beggar's Bush is the name of a tree which once stood on the left hand of the London road from Huntingdon to Caxton; so called because it was a noted rendezvous for beggars.'

Brewer's entry can be traced back to Thomas Fuller's *History of the Worthies of England* (1662) who linked the site at Godmanchester with a report of the use of the literary phrase, in an exchange between King James and Francis Bacon, saying 'it is spoken of such who use dissolute and improvident courses, which tend to poverty'. Fuller's distinctive wording was copied in several anthologies. It was conflated by Brewer with the statement that this site was a rendezvous for beggars by a Guy Miege, a French author, who also recorded Clause, King of the Beggars, as a real person. There are no local stories or records of that. The OED reproduced Brewer's explanation.

Miege probably got the name from a prominent feature on Christopher Saxton's *Five Counties' Map* (1576) where it is shown as a hill with a single tree on top. The actual site is an exposed plateau, similar to the local sites. In the early eighteenth century it became Kings Bush (perhaps ironic) and is now occupied by Wood Green Animal Rescue Centre, which has its own wind turbine on the site.

Saxton published the first series of maps of English counties. His maps were widely distributed in atlas form and as single sheets. The plates for them remained in circulation as late as 1775. They were sold through a network of chapmen in towns markets and fairs around England. In addition, the map and symbol were copied so this Beggars Bush hill appeared on almost every map of Huntingdonshire printed over the next two hundred years.

Fig 4 Extract from Saxton's 'Five Counties Map'

The earliest literary reference to the Huntingdon site is by John Taylor 'The Water Poet' in the dedication to his pamphlet *The Praise, Antiquity, and Commodity, of Beggery, Beggers & begging.* (1621). That contains a wonderful woodcut showing two ragged beggars under Beggars Bush, but bears no relationship to the poem, which is Taylor's usual doggerel and does not mention Beggars Bush. Taylor would have passed the site during his *Pennyles Pilgrimage* (1618) but makes no mention of it in that work, which suggests he was aware of it from a map.

Fig 5 The woodcut from The Praise, Antiquity, and Commodity of Beggery, Beggers, & begging (1621)

Foreign Beggars Bushes
It is impossible to prove that no beggar never took refuge under or at any sites called Beggars Bush in England, though the phrase does not appear in any of the rogue literature dealing with the Elizabethan Underworld or the many instructions to local Justices to deal with them. However, there are several sites outside England where the circumstances exclude that possibility, and the beggars are clearly good, honest people brought to poverty or worse.

1) County Offaly, Ireland – 1597
   The Dialogue of Silvynne and Peregrynne by 'H.C.' claims to be an account of part of the Nine Years War. It describes *diuers outradges*, and in particular a *whot skirmishe* at Philipstown (*Daingean*), a plantation town created to extend the Pale around Dublin. *Beggars Bush* is mentioned several times. The main reference says that the rebel band '. . . *burned the moste parte of the subberbs withowt the north gate called beggars bush to the hinderance, and undoinge of many an honest subiect*'.

2) Charles River, Virginia – 1620
   Charles City was an incorporation created by the Virginia Company, promoted as *Earth's only Paradise* by Michael Drayton. Settlers complained that the reality was *nothing but wretchedness and labour*, and the death rate for early emigrants to Virginia has been put at 80%. Samuel Jordan probably arrived in 1610. He was later granted an isolated plantation. During the uprising by the Pamunkeys in 1622 it is recorded that 'Master Samuel Iordan gathered together but a few of the straglers about him at Beggers Bush which he fortified and lived in despight of the enemy'. Recent excavations have revealed a palisade with a gatehouse, enclosing a cramped collection of wooden structures, and armour.

3) Albany, Cape Province, South Africa - 1832
   Albany Division was created as a buffer zone against the Xhosa tribes. 4,000 unprepared English emigrants arrived in the 1820s, having been told to expect something like the Home Counties. They found an area subject to drought with 'sour veldt' where the grass becomes poisonous after grazing. It was acquired in 1832 by a P. C. Daniel who had been a goldsmith (probably a moneylender) in Dublin and Soho. His mistress, who had travelled with him and his wife, appears to have lived there with their ten children; she claimed compensation for livestock and crops carried away in the 'Kaffir Wars'.

4) Suvla Bay, Gallipoli 1915
   The naming of this example can be precisely fixed between 7th August 1915 when the Royal Irish Fusiliers arrived at Suvla Bay and 1st September 1915 when Private A.J. Owens, 1st County of London Yeomanry, relieving them, was killed in action at a position called Beggars Bush. Dispatches record that the trenches 'were both narrow and shallow, and enfiladed by the enemy's guns'. Trenches were named by troops on the ground. As with trenches on the Western Front locations at Gallipoli included ironic names (Piccadilly Circus, Brighton Beach) descriptive names (Lone Pine, Scrubby Knoll and The Zig-zag) and those descriptive of the soldier's experience (Dead Man's Ridge, Hell Spit, and Rest Gully).

[1] *The Place-Names of Wiltshire* edited by J E B Gover, A. Mawer & F. M. Stenton (Cambridge, 1939) p.455.

[2] J. Field, 'Derogatory Field Names', *Journal of the English Place Name Society,* 9 (1993) pp.20-25.

[3] SRO D.615, copy Frome Museum

[4] Orchardleigh Champneys Estate papers, SRO, abstracts at Frome Museum, D.418, D.B.674.

[5] C/D436, D.B.685, Bundles 10/11.

[6] Archives of St John the Baptist Church, Frome, reference number 17.1.14.1, transcription ©2010 Richard Myers and David Smart of the Frome Research Group.

[7] The Almshouse large book of 1738 as recorded in A Crocker's Historical Account of the Almshouse and School Charities of Frome (1815)

[8] Survey of the Parish of Frome Selwood 1814 made by Jeremiah Cruse, Land Surveyor, Bath 1814, FSLS Library transcript. p.21 Cuckow Hill, p.25 Oldford.

[9] McGarvie, M. ed. *Crime and Punishment in Regency Frome: The Journals of Isaac Gregory, Constable of Frome 1813-14 and 1817-18,* 1984, Frome Society.

[10] R. Coates, 'Coldharbour – for the last time?' *Nomina.* 8 (1984) pp.73-78.

[11] A. Fox, *Oral and Literate Culture in England, 1500-1700* (Oxford, 2000)

WILLIAM BRETT HARVEY – Part Two – A Man of Many Parts

Nick Hersey

Part one of Harvey's biography in Yearbook 23 concluded with an explanation of the Band of Hope's implementation of rational recreation. Although open to all, the events discussed were predominantly intended for locals but visitors to Frome were not ignored. The Whites were running a coffee shop, with resident lodgers, in the Market Place according to the 1851 census, and this had become a temperance hotel by 1855.[104] Samuel Wilkins seems to have started another in 1858 and similar establishments can be found in Frome for many decades afterwards.[105] The most enduring was probably the Sims' hotel, where the committee of the Band of Hope took tea and enjoyed social conversation in May 1862. It was still advertising in 1919.[106]

As was the case throughout the country, soldiers were billeted in Frome inns as military circumstances dictated and the temperance movement always participated in the drive to make them welcome. In 1889 soldiers were offered free tea in the Temperance Hall, followed by a concert and addresses. Harvey 'exerted himself indefatigably in making the guests comfortable and happy'[107] and in 1914, the hall was offered for soldiers' entertainment. He added that 'if the arrangements of the Hall were not in any respect satisfactory he would be glad to receive suggestions from them'.[108] In the war years, the *Somerset & Wilts Journal (SWJ)* regularly published 'An Entertainment Directory for the Soldiers,' and the local women's temperance group sought to make billeted soldiers 'so comfortable that they would not want to go to public houses'.[109] The detailed reporting of well-attended events was a part of the teetotalists' publicity campaign.[110]

Another aspect of temperance publicity is the £1,500 that the Band of Hope raised to build a new Temperance Hall in 1874. Of course, it had a practical value as 'the acquisition of a new public place of meeting' and would be 'a great accommodation for temperance gatherings, Good Templar lodge meetings, practices of the Frome Temperance Choral Society, the meetings of the Rechabites and other benefit societies, the payment of pensioners, committee meetings etc'. It could be hired out to raise funds for the temperance movement and was also a physical symbol of the importance and strength of the local temperance organisation. Many people were involved in its planning and construction but two figures were key: Joseph Chapman, as architect and the committee member who best understood the practicalities of construction and Harvey who 'said he had done his best in getting in funds for the hall'. Chapman generously 'attributed their success mainly to the energy of Mr W B Harvey, the secretary'.[111]

Clearly, many people put a huge effort over several decades into promoting temperance. Was it all really necessary? The evidence is mixed here because temperance campaigners had concerns and motives which seem strange to many in the 21st century. We do not, as a society, see activities that are popular and legal on a Saturday as 'Sabbath desecration' if they occur on a Sunday.[112] We do not, worry about 'irreligion' in the working class, or in any other class.[113] But if indeed Harvey and his associates had a flawed analysis of the problem it does not mean that there was no problem.

Hogarth, Cruikshank, Dickens and Hugo did not invent the social problems they fictionalised. Harvey and the *SWJ* may have had an agenda but they did not invent the poverty, distress and violence in many parts of nineteenth century Frome: the drunken father who 'took by force from his children their hard-earned wages'; Naish's Street 'full of drunken and riotous people,

The Temperance Hall is just to the left of the car. Now demolished.

many of whom were women, half naked and streaming with blood'; the distressingly regular appearance of battered wives in court, withdrawing charges or pleading that their man be treated leniently because he was 'a good husband when not in beer' (and the only financial support the family had); the violent detail in what all concerned believed was Charlotte Budgett's dying deposition.[114]

People such as these would never seek out Christianity and so, from 1859, the temperance movement sought them out by commencing the Frome Temperance Mission. They employed a Mr Anderson to visit houses, leave tracts, both teetotal and religious, and hold cottage meetings in the poorer parts of town such as Duke Street and Butts Square. The *SWJ* reported this and publicised the Band of Hope committee's interest in learning of 'particular cases to which the attention of the Missionary may be usefully directed'.[115] Anderson soon had a list of 140 'degraded and hitherto sadly neglected ones' and, in a few months, the *SWJ* claimed, that half had become total abstainers and a third were attending church regularly.[116] There was, however, respectable opposition to this work, because it was arranged by a teetotal organisation. The Band of Hope responded by ceding control to a committee of the town's clerics and the Temperance Mission became the Frome Town Mission, consciously modelled on the London City Mission.[117]

It was a change in name only, but it was also the high-point of the movement. A ragged school, a girls' school and mothers' meetings were supported and the focus continued on the 'drunkenness and indifference, 'ignorance and irreligion' of the poorest areas where 'the ordinary way of preaching and pastoral visitation' failed to reach. Lodging houses were visited and tramps supplied with bibles. However, income plummeted and there was a 'sad decline in interest'. Anderson was reluctantly replaced by a cheaper Bible-woman, and the focus moved from teetotalism to morality and evangelism. It was only support from the YMCA, Quakers and the 'kindly interest of ladies' that kept it going.[118] Although funds improved during the 1870s they never returned to the level of the early 1860s.[119] Despite this persistent shortage of income, the mission continued its work into the twentieth century and Harvey continued to insist that it was a Christian's duty to support this work. He was still on the committee in 1916 and chaired a fund-raising lantern-lecture in 1918.[120] However, much of its activity by this time could be characterised as social work and many had come to realise that the Mission 'needed to do something more than simply getting the gospel preached' or it would only be 'touching the fringe of the problem and not grappling with it'.[121]

The problem, though often not clearly specified, was generally perceived to be the lifestyle of the poor. The politician's approach was (and is) to attack the issue by external legislation, imposing improvements in education, housing, health and education from above. Harvey was well aware of the necessity for campaigns to operate at a national level, even if he was never as deeply involved in party politics as he was in the temperance movement or nonconformity.

The first indication, so far discovered, of Harvey's political views comes from the 1859 general election, where a poll book shows him to have supported the Radical candidate, Donald Nicoll.[122] Despite this, he was at this stage attempting to keep the *SWJ* politically neutral.[123] Frome had something of a history of election hostilities and riot, so it is not surprising that Harvey was asking, in his paper, for 'arguments presented to the judgement and reason, rather than appeals to the physical part of our nature.'[124] From his arrival, he seems not to have attended any public political meetings for several years.

Whether the overtly campaigning nature of the *SWJ* concerning religious discrimination and temperance would ever have allowed this neutral stance to be credible is debatable.[125] As it happened the advent of the *Frome Times*, an avowedly pro-Conservative paper meant that conflict was inevitable.[126] In 1864 the *SWJ* accused 'our Tory contemporary, the *Frome Times*' of ineffectually trying to use 'wily counsels' to sow dissension in Liberal ranks. Soon afterwards it reprinted a *Weekly Dispatch* article that labelled Tories 'obsequious tools of prerogative' and accused them of 'stupidity, stolid prejudice, sordid bigotry, and insane ignorance'.[127] Harvey did not write this but, as owner and editor, he caused it to be re-published. He probably did, however, write an editorial in 1866 that protested against the ejectment of Liberal Fromian tenants by their Tory supporting landlord (Lord Bath): 'What is the Conservative idea of legitimate influence and the rights of property? The answer is plain enough — *abject slavery in mind and conscience in all who can be controlled*'. (*SWJ*'s italics).[128]

Neutrality abandoned, the following week saw Harvey reported at a political meeting. He was amongst many prominent Liberals at a Reform Meeting who escorted Frome's MP, Henry Rawlinson, to the platform and he and Henry Houston proposed one of the motions supporting government policy.[129] Similarly, in 1868, he proposed a motion pledging support to Thomas Hughes' candidacy, despite the fact that Hughes was a very different sort of Liberal candidate from his Fromian predecessors.[130] For Harvey, the important thing was to return a Liberal, even if he didn't always agree with every view of that person. Hence the motion he moved in 1873, calling for a large committee, to choose a new Liberal candidate. Harvey stressed the need to unite around a candidate who they could agree with in the main, anybody who supported Bright and Gladstone would be better than a Tory.

Interestingly, he 'put Mr Bright's name first because he had even more confidence in him than in Mr Gladstone, although Mr Gladstone was a noble man, and with Mr Bright at his side he would not go far wrong.'[131] However this attitude had reversed by 1886 when an *SWJ* editorial regretted that Bright was unable to support Gladstone over Ireland.[132] With hindsight, the Liberal Party was doomed by the advent of the Labour Party, but the fracture over Irish Home Rule also caused it harm. In Frome, Henry Carey Houston and Joseph Tanner chose the side of Unionism but most Liberals, including the wider Harvey family and Tanner's sons, sided with Gladstone's plan to end 'the distressing results of coercion' in Ireland.[133]

Although not really a political activist, Harvey regularly appeared on the platform at major meetings, sometimes simply lending his presence, but often endorsing a specific candidate or policy.[134] He was a member of various local Liberal Committees in the 1870s and 1880s and is reported nominating candidates at election time.[135] Indeed one of his last public acts in 1918 was to nominate John Barlow, who had been Frome's Liberal MP since 1896, for re-election.[136] Harvey didn't live to see the outcome of the election: Barlow came a humiliatingly distant third in a world that had changed, it seems forever.[137]

SIR J. E. BARLOW, BART.
LIBERAL CANDIDATE FOR THE FROME DIVISION.
PUBLISHED BY EAMES, STATIONER, FROME.

Sir John Barlow

On the whole Harvey's work was at the level of the individual, not the nation. He sought to encourage people to take decisions for themselves that would improve their lives. His involvement with Zion Chapel, the Band of Hope and the Mechanics' Institute were discussed in part one. Another organisation with which Harvey was 'intimately connected' in its early days was the Penny Bank which, in Frome, began life in April 1858 as The Frome Band of Hope Penny Bank. Initially its stated object was 'to encourage habits of frugal economy in the young', and it was open to all aged under twenty-one. Nonetheless, as with the Town Mission, there was hostility from some because of the titular temperance connection. Harvey defended this as a sensible limited beginning, in the footsteps of the successful York Penny Bank, and asserted that developments, including the eligibility of adults, would come only when it was clear that the bank could cope with expansion.[138] A youthful Harvey explained the benefits in an essay of 1859. The artisan's small deposit would not be 'treated with disdain' and so he would feel welcome and encouraged to save, but the venue for taking deposits would never be a pub and so he would not be exposed to temptation or to rules that insisted he buy at least one pint 'for the benefit of the host'. Once the money was deposited, the withdrawal process prevented that impulsive frittering to which money in the pocket or 'the cracked teapot' was susceptible.[139] The bank was a success, operating at least until the 1930s and the *SWJ* sometimes published deposit and withdrawal details to keep its existence and stability in the public eye.[140]

In a similar vein, Harvey always supported the Frome Mutual Benefit Society. A lengthy *SWJ* article in 1857 commends this 'admirable society,' to its readers as 'by far the most efficient society of the kind in the town'. The idea of paying in advance for sickness or death benefits accorded exactly with Harvey's world view. Moreover, the society's rules 'forbid its meetings to be held in a public house'.[141] Harvey seems not to have directly participated in the management of the society, although he was its auditor.[142] However he regularly contributed to the entertainment that leavened the business of the annual tea meeting: usually, he sang.[143]

On the other hand, he was directly involved in the running of the Frome Permanent Building Society, attending the first meeting and being a founding director in 1860 and still holding that directorial position at the outbreak of the First World War. He was chairman between May 1898 and October 1910.[144] In his chairman's address of 1901, Harvey said it was clear 'that the society was fulfilling its purpose as a helper of those of limited means... The object of the society was not to make large profits but to enable its members to build or purchase houses'. He considered the outlook for the society 'most hopeful' and concluded by referring to 'the large number of heads of families, now living in comfortable houses of their own, who acquired the habit of thrift when young men, by investing a portion of their weekly earnings in that society'.[145] Clearly he did not just have an aspiration to 'wean the working man from the beer house,' he strove throughout his life 'to advance the moral condition of the industrial classes' and to instil in them what, today, we might term middle-class values. Despite his dedication over decades, he never felt he had achieved enough. In 1906, he was still urging building society members to induce others to join: 'Young men should specially be appealed to, as the cultivation of the habit of thrift in those who had too often neglected it and had spent all their earnings without regard to future needs would prove an inestimable blessing to them'.[146]

In the minds of Harvey and many of his co-workers, the Christian faith was the foundation of their world view. 'Aggressive temperance' work was the 'duty' of the Church because 'the work of the churches and the work of the liquor traffic were in deadly antagonism'. Virtually every report of a temperance meeting in Frome had clerical involvement and speakers constantly referred to the scriptural basis of their cause and how public-houses opposed God's work. Indeed, the abstentionist philosophy that those without a drink problem must still abstain to support 'weaker brethren' and 'elevate' society is usually presented in the context of Christian duty. Harvey himself felt 'that the temperance cause was in beautiful harmony with the cause of God'.[147]

To some extent, this seems to have been the case across England, however TG Rooke (minister at Sheppards Barton Chapel and temperance activist) once claimed that the connection between religion and temperance was 'recognised by the leaders of the temperance cause in Frome, more than in any other locality he was acquainted with'.[148] So it is not surprising to find meetings opening and closing with prayers and temperance hymns being sung.[149] The Frome Band of Hope committee, always avowedly ecumenical, was eventually joined by some of those evangelically inclined Church of England adherents and proudly claimed to 'collectively represent every denomination of Christians in the town'.[150] The connection was even clearer by the 1880s, with the rise of the White Ribbon Army, a regional vehicle for the gospel temperance movement. In 1882, Harvey presided at a gospel temperance meeting and expressed his 'hearty sympathy with the White Ribbon Army in the good work they were doing for Temperance in the town'. He was still presiding at meetings and showing his support in the twentieth century.[151]

As in the early temperance years there were yobbish attempts to disrupt meetings, but Frome had learnt. The Band of Hope committee, led in this matter by ST Rawlings and a 'large staff of efficient assistants... admirably seconded by the police, nipped in the bud all attempts at misconduct'.[152] With illegitimate opposition suppressed, meetings soon moved outdoors, taking the message to the people. The Mint was one favourite venue, Broad Street another.[153] There are clear similarities here between the work of White Ribbon Army and that of the Salvation Army. From 1882, the *SWJ* was overt in its support for the work of the Salvation Army and Harvey was still showing his personal support by chairing a meeting in 1916.[154] Harvey thought the work of the Salvation Army 'one of the wonders of the world'. General Booth had seen a problem outside the London gin-palaces and had actually done something. By the twentieth century, thousands volunteered or 'worked for the merest pittance, giving up their lives for the sake of their fellows'. It was the 'Christlike' practical nature of this 'social work... such as food depots, shelters... police-court mission... the rescue of fallen women, inebriates' homes, hospitals and nurses for young mothers, lodging houses, midnight meetings' that caused Harvey to 'commend the work to Christian people'. In 1906 he felt it 'a great honour and privilege to welcome a man such as General Booth to their town'.[155]

It is easy to see these 'armies' as more modern and dynamic versions of the Town Mission and therefore to understand why Harvey valued all three. As well as selling their publications, he was treasurer and secretary of the local auxiliary of the Religious Tract Society for fifteen years.[156] He resigned in 1914 'not due to declining interest but to his inability to do what he wished to do'.[157] It was probably his interest in rational recreation that led Harvey to be treasurer of the local YMCA from its inception. His support is clear from the *SWJ*'s reporting of the first exploratory meeting: 'we earnestly commend the movement to the sympathy, prayers and co-operation not only of the young men of the town but of the Christian community at large'. As with the building of the Temperance Hall, he seems to have been the organiser of the fundraising in connection with the purchase and extension of their own meeting room in High Street. By 1910 he was president and is last reported chairing a joint meeting with The Brotherhood in July 1914.[158]

Perhaps the most impressive of Harvey 's building achievements was the Jubilee Baths: it was not a simple process. The collective worthies of Frome assembled at the Police Court on 12 February 1863 to discuss how best to celebrate the forthcoming marriage of the Prince of Wales. As well as the usual ideas of a parade or a dinner for the poor, there was much interest in the concept of a public baths. A genuinely cross-party and cross-religion committee, was set up 'to make the necessary arrangements'.[159] This committee included both Harvey and WC Penny (co-owner and co-publisher of the *Frome Times*) so it is not surprising that the local press was supportive of the concept. Unfortunately, whilst there was general enthusiasm for a public bath, there was no agreement as to what that actually meant. So while the *SWJ*'s editorial described the plans as 'most complete' and including a swimming bath, the *Frome Times* reported that the Rev A Daniel and Mr WC Penny thought the idea of a swimming bath 'useless'.[160] The scheme was abandoned and revived at least twice in 1863 before finally foundering on the impracticalities of the sites available, the insufficiency of the water supply and the intransigence of grocer John Blackwell, one of the leading exponents and a man previously castigated by the *SWJ* for his 'self-laudatory perversion of the truth'.[161]

Over the years there were occasional mentions of the desirability of public baths, but Frome largely forgot about the idea until 1887.[162] Even then the committee for a permanent memorial to the Queen's Golden Jubilee (including Harvey) agreed that a recreation ground was the best option. The Swimming Club swam in the river, as people always had, and many thought this perfectly adequate, not to mention free. However, a spate of drownings in the late 1880s led individuals, including Harvey, to write letters in favour of a public baths. Coroner Muller, at an inquest, said that Frome had a reputation for drowning accidents and he hoped it would soon have a large swimming baths.[163] Throughout 1891 support for public baths on Frome's rates seemed to be building, but again it came to nothing.[164]

The idea emerged again in February 1897, when the need for a permanent memorial celebrating Victoria's Diamond Jubilee was raised. The Urban District Council (UDC) called a public meeting at which two ideas commanded much support: a new hospital, including provision for a nurses' home, and public baths for swimming and washing. There seemed more support, by those most able to afford subscriptions, for a new hospital. Harvey and others argued that the Cottage Hospital was more than adequate for current needs and that, in the absence of a safe public bathing facility, the need for this was more pressing. A committee, including Harvey, was elected to investigate all the possibilities and report back.[165]

The Jubilee itself came and went, with Harvey running a successful fireworks display.[166] Amidst letters to the press and allegations of bad faith and fake news, it was decided to build both a new hospital and a public baths, although the final subscription list suggested insufficient funds for either scheme, let alone both.[167] The Jubilee Committee voted itself out of existence at the end of January 1898 and Harvey found himself chairman of a Baths Committee that still couldn't agree on what it wanted to build, although Harvey himself was strongly committed to swimming baths.[168]

There is no clear development of ideas reported in the press, but matters moved rapidly at this point. There was a general assumption that, once built by subscriptions, the baths would be handed over to the UDC to run and maintain. As with the earlier development of the recreation ground, Philip Edinger, surveyor to the UDC, volunteered to draw up plans for the Baths Committee. This virtually guaranteed the acceptance of the plans and many candidates for election to the UDC mentioned their support for a baths' scheme in their manifestos. Harvey himself had flatly refused to serve when nominated for the Local Board in 1865. In 1898 he declined to campaign but agreed to serve if voters indicated their approval of his record and came ninth out of the fifteen successful candidates.[169]

At the end of May the Baths Committee announced that the baths would be built on part of the former site of Cockey's Foundry, behind the cottages in Bath Street. The site was chosen for its central location, with access from Bath Street along Rook Lane and also from Sheppard's Barton. Another great advantage was that it would be considerably cheaper to adapt an existing building, rather than build anew. Nonetheless at least another £500 in donations was needed and a finance committee was set up to monitor assets and expenditure and plan fund-raising. Harvey was chairman of both committees.[170]

The whole committee, worked very hard over a long period to bring the project to fruition. Harvey 's was the experienced guiding hand whilst relative youngsters such as TH Woodland (by this time co-owner of the *SWJ*) did more of the leg work. From July 1898 the work proceeded apace, despite funding still being needed, and many individuals and organisations made generous contributions.[171] An entertainment by Frome's Volunteer Fire Brigade barely made any profit but several open days and the support of the press generated much interest in the three day 'Norwegian Bazaar' which raised £479 16s 7d.[172] At this stage, Baths Committee members Harvey and JW Singer were both also Urban District Councillors and so were well-placed to progress the adoption of the Baths by the UDC. They proposed and seconded the formal adoption motion in April 1899 and both were then elected onto the UDC's Baths Committee.[173]

Frome's Baths were adopted by the council and formally opened on 18th May 1899, just twelve months after construction work began.[174] However Harvey's connection with them continued for the rest of his life. He was chairman of the UDC's Baths Committee for many years and after retiring from public office was chairman of the Baths Improvement Committee and regularly re-elected as an honorary vice-president of the Swimming Club.[175] His consistent support for public baths reflected his belief in healthy exercise and recreation and his determination that Frome's facility should be 'well used by both sexes of all ages' led him to support and achieve mixed family bathing sessions when others were concerned at possible impropriety.[176]

Only on the question of Sunday bathing did Harvey show himself out of step with changing attitudes. At a meeting on 15 May 1899, he expressed his opposition to Sunday work and explained that that was why he had argued at the UDC against opening the baths on Sunday. Even the Reverend James Walker of Sheppard's Barton could not convince him otherwise, and Sunday closure undoubtedly had some local support. However, the UDC changed its mind the following year and voted, by nine votes to four, to allow Sunday opening between 7:00am and 9:00am.[177] A similar council debate was held in 1901, at which it emerged that demand on Sunday was being suppressed by the strangely high prices charged on that day. ER Trotman also pointed out that since the baths closed at 9:00am, anyone who wished could still attend a place of worship. It was decided to continue Sunday opening but reduce the charge from 6d to 2d.[178] Again, in 1902, the Baths Committee, under Harvey, proposed to end Sunday opening. They produced specious statistics concerning Sunday usage to support their case but were forced to admit that since they had no idea how many season ticket holders attended, they had no idea how many swam on a Sunday. The UDC seemed more impressed by both the personal observation of councillor Fred Weeks that the number of swimmers on a Sunday was three or four times higher than the committee suggested and also by the memorial against Sunday closing from 213 swimmers. JW Singer urged his fellow councillors to pay no attention to 'narrow minded gentlemen' and the UDC voted to continue Sunday opening by nine votes to six.[179] The matter was never raised again.

It is a fine line, and often a matter of opinion, where perseverance and adherence to principle end and dogmatic intransigence begins. Harvey was not usually held to be narrow minded, but at the same time that he was annoying people over Sunday bathing he was also deemed by many to be exceedingly annoying concerning beer in the workhouse.

Harvey was citing intemperance as a major contributor to workhouse numbers at least by 1892, although the idea had been a teetotaller's commonplace for decades.[180] His one term as a Guardian of the Poor began in 1901, the year in which he disposed of the remainder of his businesses.[181] As with the UDC, Harvey claimed to have been nominated without his knowledge. Nonetheless, he agreed to serve if his experience and 'intense sympathy with the poor' appealed to electors. He was comfortably elected, his 603 votes being very close in number to the 618 votes that re-elected him to the UDC.[182] Even before his accession, Guardian LW Vallis had questioned whether the doctor's prescriptions of beer for some inmates were really 'necessary', but alcoholic controversy was avoided until November 1901.[183] At this point, the Guardians received a circular from the Executive of the National United Temperance Council, urging Frome to ban alcohol as part of the Workhouse Christmas meal. Only Harvey showed any interest in the contents and the circular was ignored. Nonetheless Harvey chose to resurrect the issue at the next meeting, arguing that whilst gifts of beer were well-intentioned, they were ill-judged. Many inmates of workhouses, he asserted, were weak; many others had inherited weakness from their parents. It was therefore in the interest of comfort and good discipline to align with two hundred other workhouses around the country and prohibit the usual two distributions of a half-pint of beer to each inmate who requested it. In total, eight guardians supported this proposition but sixteen agreed with those who said that Harvey's arguments were cruel, coercive and unnecessary.[184]

There was no dispute over beer for the inmates at the time of the coronation of Edward VII, possibly because Harvey was not at the meeting that agreed it.[185] However he again attempted to prohibit beer in the workhouse for Christmas 1902. Whilst he obviously had his supporters, a clear majority of the meeting disbelieved his assertion that this was a matter of the Guardian's duty and not a teetotal issue. The Rev Walker objected to having 'to hear a teetotal sermon from Mr Harvey,' Mr Hayman said Harvey lacked 'decency,' maligned the inmates and was wasting the Guardians' time. Mr Hood-Wright accused Harvey of 'a libel' on the inmates, while Mr Parfitt reported attending Christmas dinner 'on many years' and seeing no wrong. Harvey lost the issue by nineteen votes to eight.[186]

The *SWJ* condemned some Guardians' behaviour, while readers protested the treatment of 'one of the most honoured men in Frome'. Frome's Band of Hope placed an advertisement commending 'their esteemed President Mr W B Harvey for his manly and patriotic effort to shield the inmates of the Frome workhouse... from the temptations inseparably connected with the use of strong drink'. They also protested 'the ungentlemanly and unchristian manner in which his proposal was received'.[187] The *Somerset Standard* did not carry this advertisement but it did carry letters disagreeing with Harvey's actions. Particularly telling was the assertion that Harvey's 'narrow and bigoted views... have materially helped to render... unpopular and distasteful... the cause of temperance... which should commend itself to every right-thinking person'.[188] This, in a nutshell, is a major reason why the total abstinence movement (as the temperance movement is more accurately called) failed. Offended citizens, convinced of their own morality, rejected attempts by others to annex the moral high ground: and there were more of the offended than there were supporters of the temperance movement.

Harvey tried again to prohibit the acceptance of alcoholic gifts for Christmas 1903 'because it is a matter of conviction with me' but lost by thirteen votes to six.[189] He also lost his seat in the 1904 election, although he retained his place on the UDC. He polled several dozen fewer votes, compared to 1901, in both elections, although his defeat as a Guardian was narrow.[190] Nonetheless, in both elections, he stood on his record and in asking voters for a renewal of their confidence 'If my conduct has received your approval' he received a rebuff.[191] However it would be wrong to let his mistaken persistence detract from the great good Harvey did through his decades of involvement with the workhouse.

Perhaps because they didn't want to interfere with Emma Sheppard's work, the Band of Hope didn't actually hold a meeting at the workhouse until April 1869, although they did include the workhouse children in the fete parade and give them free admission to the fete with lemonade and plum cake in 1861.[192] The reporting of this first meeting, at which Harvey presided, shows how many of his interests came together in this sphere. A lecture was given and temperance songs sung. At the end the adults were given copies of the *British Workman* in the hope that they might be helped to reform whilst the children were given copies of the *Band of Hope Review* and loaned hymn books for a singalong, thus pointing them to both temporal and spiritual salvation. Lacking positive parental role models, these children saw and heard recitations by children of their own age as well as a lecture by the, relatively, youthful William John Harvey. The upbeat reporting makes clear the wholesome fun that was had by all and is interestingly egalitarian in its conclusion that 'it would be difficult to say whether the audience or the visitors will look forward to the next meeting with more pleasure'.[193]

The meetings were soon considered a success on all sides and from 1870 were supplemented by treats for the children which were similar in style to the Whitsun treats that Sunday Schools gave their members: games, food and 'fire balloons' or fireworks. In 1871 visiting lecturer William Dunn (the reformed clown, not the local solicitor) gave a special address at the workhouse and later an elocution competition was held and the prize winners' names appeared in the *SWJ*, in exactly the same way as happened after a Band of Hope meeting. This trend was continued in 1873 when, following an excellent tea, the inmates and selected guests such as the Le Gros family were entertained to a concert. Mrs WH Penny played the piano and sang whilst Harvey conducted the choir and sang several songs, both solo and in groups. The entire programme was printed in the *SWJ* just as were the usual temperance counter-attraction entertainments in town.[194] Society was moving to normalise the experience of workhouse children, which is why they lived in the separate Whitewell Home from 1913: Harvey and Frome's Band of Hope were very much a part of this change.[195] The pattern of events described above should, in broad, be considered as routine background to the further improvements described below.[196]

By the end of the 1870s, Harvey was personally supplying lemonade for juveniles and abstainers as an alternative to the beer that was supplied by J and T Baily as a workhouse Christmas treat. This personal contribution continued annually until at least 1916.[191] His provision of a fireworks treat in November was more short-lived, sadly, as killjoys amongst the Guardians decided that it was unsafe.[198] Happily the workhouse band was a longer lasting initiative and again this was a Band of Hope idea, Harvey and William John Harvey being amongst the initial subscribers. The workhouse master also made a personal donation.[199] Not only did the workhouse boys have the same musical opportunities as their town peers, it also gave numerous opportunities, mostly in the summer, to leave the workhouse and play at various fetes, treats and entertainments.[200] Playing in a band did not just provide fun, it provided opportunities and valuable experience. Hence, in his report on and to the Guardians in 1901, the government inspector said: 'the number of boys they had been able to send out to army bands especially was very gratifying as it gave them a good career in which many of them were, he understood, doing well'.[201]

By 1891, Harvey had begun his regular response to Russell Tanner's appeal that 'cast-off literature' be supplied to Frome's Workhouse as a 'boon conferred upon a class to whose lot a very large share of the ills of life have fallen'.[202] In the twentieth century, as he reduced the level of his commitments, he put more of his own time and money into the workhouse. He 'treated the children to the Aquatic Sports held at the Swimming Baths,' supplied buns for the children every Easter, and organised and led outings for the inmates of the infirmary and of course the children. The children's outings typically comprised a charabanc ride, a walk to a view point and games, singing and plenty of food.[203] In a Guardians' meeting of 1914, 'Thanks were voted to Mr W B Harvey for taking a party of old people from the House to Shearwater... [and] for his very great kindness to the old people. The Rev R W Baker said that Mr Harvey had been a very good friend to the Workhouse people. The Master (Mr W H Tapp) [added]: 'He does a great deal for them that is not formally reported to the Board'.[204]

Harvey's death certificate describes him simply as a 'retired chemist' but he was a man of surprisingly many parts. 'He had a heart that rejoiced in everything that was good' and was a 'fine example of never growing weary in well-doing'.[205] He was elected a trustee of the

Mechanics Hall, the Temperance Hall, and Zion Chapel property and assets. At least five people asked him to be an executor of their will. Acts such as these demonstrate how widely people respected and trusted 'their indomitable friend Mr W B Harvey who stood fair and square to every wind that blew'.[206] His organisational skills were widely acknowledged.[207] People relied on his integrity, his indefatigable exertions and his 'great mental ability'.[208] Shirley's Temperance Hotel in London deemed him famous and respected enough to use his testimonial in their advertising.[209] So whether as a delegate to a county church meeting, or a regional poor law conference, the spokesman for a deputation to licensing magistrates, an attendee at the World Temperance Conference of 1900, a member of the executive of the Western Temperance League or as 'one of those who had the honour to meet Asquith' to discuss licensing legislation, Harvey was the man people chose to represent them.[210]

Another quality of his that deserves mention is his tolerance and broad church approach, typified by his presidency of the Frome Sunday School Union, his willingness to attend and chair meetings at 'sister' churches and his belief that all Christians are 'co-workers in the Master's vineyard'.[211] Unlike some Dissenters, this non-denominational approach enabled him to be comfortable working with Church of England members, hoping that joint meetings 'would have the result of removing intolerance, which he always regretted'.[212] Unusually for the times he was able to unreservedly condemn the Tractarian beliefs and practices of Frome's Reverend WJE Bennett whilst respecting and even admiring the personal qualities of the man.

At Bennett's death the *SWJ* said: 'Holding as we do a view of the Christian Church the very opposite of that held by our deceased friend, we can yet honour his fidelity to conscience, and his persistence, in spite of all opposition and regardless of personal injury, in holding and teaching that which he believed to be God's truth'.[213] This mindset does much to explain his persistence in unpopular causes when a UDC Councillor and a Guardian of the Poor. Harvey could even accept a blunt personal attack. Recounting the tale of the handbills which his uncle, Lazarus Bewsey, had circulated, upbraiding the 'infidel scorners of God's good things' and taking 'this course to condemn him and his teetotal doctrines,' Harvey simply said that 'he and his uncle were very good friends after that, for they understood one another well'.[214]

It would seem only reasonable, therefore, to offer the same level of respect in return to Harvey for his sincerity and fidelity to conscience, even if many of his views are not in 'accordance with our own'. Arthur Coombs in his 'Appreciation' said that Harvey's life was one 'which all Frome men will own to have been the life of one of our heroes of peace'.[215] The *Somerset Standard's* tribute was equally respectful: 'Modest and unassuming, gentlemanly and happy, he passed on his course in life, exercising a remarkable direct influence, and with secondary results none can estimate'.[216]

Errata. In part one of this article YB 23 Page 61 line 22 should read £200 not £2

NB. All references are all available via publications@fsls.org.uk

FROME MPs (PART 1: 1832-1885)

David Lassman

This is the first of a three-part series detailing all the Members of Parliament that have represented Frome since the election of its first MP, in 1832. In this article, those who represented the town during its time as a parliamentary borough are detailed.

Until the early 1830s, Frome was represented in Parliament simply as part of the county of Somerset and those in the town eligible to vote had to travel to Wells to cast it. With the Great Reform Act of 1832, however, all this changed. Frome was created a parliamentary borough and became entitled to return one Member of Parliament (MP) to the House of Commons. This new borough consisted only of the town of Frome and according to the census taken the previous year, had a population of just over 11,200. Out of these, there was a registered electorate of 322 – which consisted almost exclusively of men of property, wealth, and distinction.

Despite this small electorate there was great excitement in the town accompanying these reforms. Representatives of various trades in the town, accompanied by bands and banners, marched to Bath, where there was a great rally addressed by various politicians. Back in Frome, a bonfire was lit in the Market Place and in Willow Vale an ox was roasted whole.

The first Frome election took place in December 1832. There were two candidates who stood for the seat – Mr Thomas Sheppard and Sir Thomas Champneys – both of whom were well-known local figures and members of established families of the town – the Sheppards of Fromefield and the Champneys of Orchardleigh. There had been bad blood between the two families for many years and this contest would be no different. The election lasted three days and was accompanied on each by rioting. On the first day, 10 December 1832, the candidates were nominated, and speeches were made from the hustings, which had been erected outside The George Hotel, in the Market Place.

Thomas Sheppard, representing the Whigs, was pelted with stones 'and other missiles' while making his speech, and fighting broke out between his supporters and followers of the Tory Champneys. Although numerous special constables were sworn-in, it was not enough to quell the rioting, and so the magistrates sent a message to Trowbridge for the Dragoons to assist. Despite this military intervention, Sheppard and his companions were forced out of town and took refuge in his brother's house at Fromefield, where a siege mentality existed for the remainder of the election. When the dust eventually settled, and the polling was complete, Sheppard could claim victory by a majority of 63 votes; having beaten Champneys by 163 to 100, with an 81.7% turnout of the electorate brave enough to call out their votes (secret ballots would not arrive for more than four decades). Thomas Sheppard became Frome's first Member of Parliament.

This would be Champneys only attempt at becoming an MP, but Sheppard would contest a further three elections. The first of these, in January 1835, saw Sheppard taking on two opponents – Matthew Bridges (Radical) and Courtenay Boyle (Whig) – with Sheppard by now having crossed the floor to represent the Conservatives. Although the turnout was slightly down, as was his majority, he retained his seat quite comfortably, but things would be a lot closer two years later.

104

In 1837, with an election triggered by the death of William IV, Sheppard was again opposed by Courtenay Boyle, who had come third in the previous election. The Whig candidate was a member of another famous family in the area – the Boyles. The family lived at Marston House, near Frome, and in 1620 had had the title of Earl of the County of Cork bestowed upon them, which was then later held in conjunction with the Earldom of Orrery. Admiral Sir Courtenay Boyle, as he would later become, was the son of Edmund Boyle, the 7th Earl of Cork and Orrery. Although Sheppard claimed victory, the majority was a mere four votes (124 to 120) this victory is alleged to have cost him in the region of £10,000 in bribes. Four years later, a sole Whig once again opposed Sheppard, but this time a 25 majority saw off Mr William Sturch, whose commendable 129 votes was not enough to beat Sheppard's 154. This would be the last election Thomas Sheppard would contest and he stood down in 1847.

After ten years of being Conservative (Sheppard's first term as MP was, of course, as a Whig), the town went Liberal with the election of unopposed Whig, Robert Edward Boyle. Boyle was the fourth son of Edmund Boyle, 8th Earl of Cork and Orrery. He was a soldier and served with the Coldstream Guards, where he achieved the rank of colonel. Having been returned unopposed in 1847, he repeated this feat in the 1852 election, although not without controversy. As Secretary of the Order of St Patrick he was paid by the Government and thereby, so it was argued, disqualified as an MP. He was returned unopposed, but the issue would not go away and after an electoral petition, the result was voided, and a by-election called. Boyle resigned from the Order of St. Patrick, presented himself for re-election, and was returned unopposed. His tenure would be just as short-lived though, as the following year he resigned to join his regiment, on their way to the Crimea. He never reached the fighting, as he died of fever at Varna, on 3 September 1854 and was buried at sea.

The resignation of Boyle meant that another by-election was called and this took place in October 1854. This time a vote would be required, as there were two candidates, although somewhat bizarrely, both were in effect Liberals. The first of these was a Radical Liberal, Mr Donald Nicoll who was well-known for his business connections with the town and was popular with the working class. He alleged that the previous MP – Robert Boyle – had made a pact with him to the effect that he, Nicoll, would succeed him as the Liberal candidate. However, Boyle's nephew, Richard Edmund St Lawrence Boyle, Lord Dungarvan, decided that he wanted to retain the family's connection to the Frome seat.

In a bitterly contested battle – which saw Richard Boyle receiving Tory support, while non-conformist ministers rallied around Nicoll – Boyle was victorious, gaining a 52-vote majority, with the largest turnout percentage (84.9%) in Frome's short voting history: this equated to 310 voters out of a possible registered electorate of 365. Boyle having secured 181 of them, to Nicoll's 129. Angry scenes followed Nicoll's defeat, with the windows of the George Hotel – Boyle's headquarters – being broken by the loser's supporters. The Riot Act was read from the hotel's balcony and the Yeomanry was called out to restore peace.

Donald Nicoll stood again, two years later, in another by-election, this time triggered by Richard Boyle's elevation to the House of Lords on the death of his grandfather, the 8th Earl of Cork & Orrery. Nicoll's opponent this time was Richard's brother, William George Boyle. Like his uncle, Robert Edward Boyle, he too was a soldier with the Coldstream Guards, eventually achieving the rank of Lieutenant-Colonel. This would be the fourth election within five years in Frome and took place on 23 July 1856.

The 1856 Frome by-election was probably the most exciting and closest run contest in the history of Frome's parliamentary status. Ultimately it would be a straight fight between two candidates, but initially there were three. At the beginning of July, Donald Nicoll, still standing as a Radical Liberal, issued his address to the electors. Two days later, Lord Edward Thynne followed suit. He was the uncle of the late Marquis of Bath and declared himself a Conservative. The Thynne estate was at nearby Longleat, across the county border in Wiltshire, although they were very strongly connected with Frome, owning much of land and property in the town. Within a week of this declaration, William George Boyle entered the race.

At a subsequent Conservative meeting a resolution was carried suggesting to Thynne that he withdraw from the contest, as the greater part of the Conservative electors were pledged to Major Boyle but his response was to go to the poll regardless. The nominations took place on Monday 21 July 1856. Mr Bush proposed Mr Donald Nicoll, while a Mr H P Coombs seconded his nomination. Mr James Hurd nominated Lord Edward Thynne, and this was seconded by a Mr Hooper. Local magistrate and successful businessman, Mr John Sinkins proposed Major Boyle and the equally well-known Mr John Webb Singer seconded.

Nicoll was declared elected by a show of hands, whereupon a poll was demanded by Hurd on behalf of Lord Thynne and Mr Miller on behalf of Major Boyle. Sometime during the day, however, Lord Thynne retired from the contest, leaving the two remaining candidates to battle it out through a vote. Nothing could prepare those gathered for the excitement that would be generated throughout the afternoon. The votes for each man – Nicoll and Boyle – were equal and as each further one was cast and counted, so the total would shift in favour of one or the other.

When the polling station closed at four o'clock in the afternoon, the impression of the densely packed crowd in the Market Place and up both Bath Street and Stoney Street, was that Mr Nicoll was ahead and would be declared elected for the second time that day. However, when the result was finally announced, not long after voting had finished, it was Major Boyle's name who was called out. It was by the narrowest of margins though, with Boyle receiving 158 to Nicoll's 157. This meant there was a majority of just one to Boyle. This proved too much for many of Nicoll's supporters, who felt victory had been snatched away from them and it was said that many normally strong men burst out crying and several sobbed aloud. They were left with their grief and to rue the fact that if Lord Thynne had not withdrawn, many of Boyle's votes would have stayed with his Lordship and Nicoll would have been assured of victory.

If the assumption that Nicoll would have won if Lord Thynne had remained in the contest sounded like sour grapes on behalf of his supporters, they were to have their belief tested eight months later, and find it vindicated. The 1857 General Election saw the three men who had contested the previous year's by-election – Nicoll, Boyle, and Thynne – all put their names forward again as candidates. With Boyle's previous voters now split between his own candidature and that of Edward Thynne, it was perhaps unsurprising Donald Nicoll, at the third time of asking, was finally elected as the Member of Parliament for Frome, receiving 162 votes, compared to Boyle's 92 and 72 of Lord Thynne.

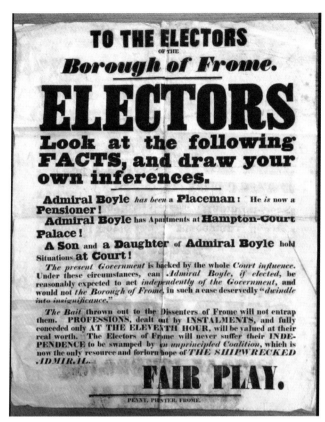

TO THE ELECTORS
OF THE

Borough of Frome.

ELECTORS

Look at the following FACTS, and draw your own inferences.

Admiral Boyle *has been* a **Placeman**! He *is* now a **Pensioner**!

Admiral Boyle has Apartments at **Hampton-Court Palace**!

A Son and a **Daughter** of **Admiral Boyle** hold Situations at **Court**!

The present Government is backed by the whole Court influence. Under these circumstances, can Admiral Boyle, if elected, be reasonably expected to act independently of the Government, and would not the Borough of Frome, in such a case deservedly "dwindle into insignificance."

The Bait thrown out to the Dissenters of Frome will not entrap them. PROFESSIONS, dealt out by INSTALMENTS, and fully conceded only AT THE ELEVENTH HOUR, will be valued at their real worth. The Electors of Frome will never suffer their INDE-PENDENCE to be swamped by an unprincipled Coalition, which is now the only resource and forlorn hope of *THE SHIPWRECKED ADMIRAL.*

FAIR PLAY.

PENNY, PRINTER, FROME.

Nicoll's time as Frome MP lasted two years, until the General Election of 1859. With the contest being once more a straight two-candidate race – Nicoll and Thynne being the candidates – Nicoll lost his seat to Thynne and the 70 majority the Radical Whigs had enjoyed in 1857, now become a 47 majority for the Conservatives: a massive 34.8% swing, with an 88.6% turnout. Thynne returned to the House of Commons, after an absence of 26 years, having been MP for the rotten borough of Weobley back in 1831 (this being swept away with the reform act the following year).

In contrast to the many elections and by-elections of the 1850s, the 1860s turned out to be the complete opposite, with no elections held for the first five years of that decade and Edward Thynne going about his business as Frome MP with no real political obstructions whatsoever. On a personal level, however, things could not be more different. Although given £20,000 by his father in 1830 (equivalent to around two million in today's money) by the time he was elected for this second time, he had been sued by creditors, received another £60,000 (more than £6 million) to clear his debts and had, after being cut off by his family, spent time in a debtor's prison.

This would be Thynne's only term as Frome MP, when the 1865 election was called, his place was taken by James Whalley Dawe Thomas Wickham. Despite the impressive name, Wickham lost the election to the Liberal Henry Rawlinson, by 23 votes. Rawlinson was a British East India Company army officer and would later be described as the father of Assyriology – the archaeological, historical, and linguistic study of Assyria and the rest of ancient Mesopotamia and of the related cultures that used cuneiform writing. Like Thynne, he had previously been an MP (representing Reigate for a brief period in 1858) and like his predecessor, would serve only one term in Frome.

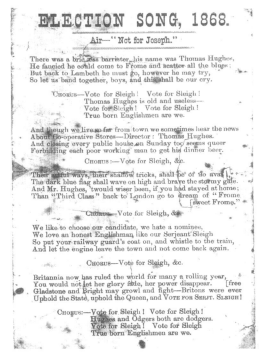

ELECTION SONG, 1868.

Air—"Not for Joseph."

There was a brie...less barrister, his name was Thomas Hughes,
He fancied he could come to Frome and scatter all the blues;
But back to Lambeth he must go, however he may try,
So let us band together, boys, and this shall be our cry.

CHORUS—Vote for Sleigh! Vote for Sleigh!
Thomas Hughes is old and useless—
Vote for Sleigh! Vote for Sleigh!
True born Englishmen are we.

And though we live so far from town we sometimes hear the news
About Co-operative Stores—Director: Thomas Hughes.
And closing every public house on Sunday too seems queer
Forbidding each poor working man to get his dinner beer.

CHORUS :—Vote for Sleigh, &c.

Their artful ways, their shallow tricks, shall be of no avail
The dark blue flag shall wave on high and brave the stormy gale.
And Mr. Hughes, 'twould wiser been, if you had stayed at home;
Than "Third Class" back to London go to dream of "Frome"
[sweet Frome."

CHORUS—Vote for Sleigh, &c.

We like to choose our candidate, we hate a nominee,
We love an honest Englishman like our Serjeant Sleigh
So put your railway guard's coat on, and whistle to the train,
And let the engine leave the town and not come back again.

CHORUS—Vote for Sleigh, &c.

Britannia now has ruled the world for many a rolling year,
You would not let her glory fade, her power disappear. [free
Gladstone and Bright may growl and fight—Britons were ever
Uphold the State, uphold the Queen, and VOTE FOR SERJT. SLEIGH!

CHORUS:—Vote for Sleigh! Vote for Sleigh!
Hughes and Odgers both are dodgers.
Vote for Sleigh! Vote for Sleigh
True born Englishmen are we.

The Liberals retained the Frome seat in the next general election, which took place in 1868, but there would be a new name on the candidate's sheet – that of Thomas Hughes. Before this, in 1867, came the Second Reform Act. Although not the degree of change the Chartists had advocated, the number of those eligible to vote increased substantially and the registered number of Frome voters rose to more than 1250, four times the amount at its first election, 35 years before.

When the preliminary meeting of the Frome Liberal Union was held in the grounds of John Sinkin's house, in Wallbridge, both Sir Henry Rawlinson and Thomas Hughes – MPs for Frome and Lambeth, respectively – were in attendance. A resolution was passed that expressed confidence in Rawlinson as member for Frome and pledged itself to return him again at the next election. Shortly after, however, Rawlinson was obliged to resign his parliamentary seat as he had accepted a seat in the Council of India. It was now that Hughes stepped into his place, having written to the committee in Lambeth, advising them of his intention to stand for Frome.

Thomas Hughes was a lawyer, judge, and politician, but is probably best known as the author of *Tom Brown's Schooldays*. Set in Rugby School, which Hughes had attended, the work is semi-autobiographical and was followed by the (lesser known) sequel, *Tom Brown at Oxford*. His opponent at the 1868 election was Conservative William Campbell Sleigh, who was also a lawyer. Sleigh would stand for office four times but never successfully. He had tried for Hughes current constituency, Lambeth, back in 1862, and Huddersfield earlier in 1868. Frome would see his third defeat, while two years later he would unsuccessfully stand for Newark. Hughes, however, would follow his Lambeth victory with another in Frome, securing a 95 majority from an 82.6% turnout.

Hughes' six years as Frome MP was marked by his controversial support of the Elementary Education Act of 1870. To what degree this affected his decision not to stand in 1874 election is open to conjecture, but whatever the reason, he left the town and stood for Marylebone instead, although he dropped out just before the election.

With Hughes' departure, the nine-year liberal reign in Frome came to an end, as through the victorious candidate Henry Lopes, the seat swung back to the Conservatives. Lopes was Member of Parliament for Launceston prior to standing for Frome. Out of the nearly 1200 voters who turned out in the 1874 election (the first in which their vote was kept secret) Lopes enjoyed an eighty-five majority, receiving 642 votes to the 557 of his liberal opponent William Henry Willans.

The By-Election of 1876 (note the 'Cheese & Grain', centre background)

When Lopes was appointed a judge two years later, in 1876, his resignation as Frome MP triggered a by-election and the resultant vote saw the town swing back to the Liberals, in the form of Henry Samuelson, previously MP for Cheltenham, having won it at the 1868 general election, but had been defeated at the following one, in 1874. Success shone on him again in Frome, and his victory against Conservative, James Fergusson by a 93 majority, would see him remain MP here for the next nine years, being returned unopposed in the 1880 election.

Samuelson would also be the last MP of the Frome parliamentary borough, as when the 1885 general election occurred the borough was abolished, and the name transferred to a new county division. The expected dramatic increase in the size of the town anticipated at the 1832 foundation of the borough had not materialised, and so by the time of the Third Reform Act, Frome was too small to continue as a constituency and the borough was abolished with effect from the 1885 election.

The new county division into which the town was placed consisted of the whole north-eastern corner of Somerset, except Bath, and was named after the town, as The Frome Division of Somerset. This would exist for the next sixty-five years and the Members of Parliament who represented it during this period will be covered in the next edition of the Frome Society Yearbook.

FROME MPS (1832-1885)

1832-47 Thomas Sheppard (Whig/Conservative)
1847-54 Robert Boyle (Whig)
1854-56 Richard Boyle (Whig)
1856-57 William Boyle (Whig)
1857-59 Donald Nicoll (Radical)
1859-65 Edward Thynne (Conservative)
1865-68 Henry Rawlinson (Liberal)
1868-74 Thomas Hughes (Liberal)
1874-76 Henry Lopes (Conservative)
1876-85 Henry Samuelson (Liberal)

SELECTED SOURCES

Elections in Frome 1832-1859 - Michael McGarvie (Frome Yearbook Vol. 18 p 41)
A Spy in the Congregation of St John's Church by ALM (Frome Yearbook Vo.18 p 45)
The Making of Frome Peter Belham ps 27-31 (1985 Frome Society)

Train to Weymouth

THE SINGERS PROJECT

Sheila Gore

Over the last two years volunteers have been working at Frome Museum as part of the Singer Conservation Project. The aim of the project is to conserve the over 3000 glass photographic negatives that were taken by the art metal work company based in Frome. This has been a stop start process to comply with the lock down regulations around Covid. In 2019 a key part of the Frome Festival was a celebration of the life and work of J W Singer, owner of the factory. The book *Casting the World* by Sue Bucklow accompanied the exhibition of the same name at Rook Lane during the festival and a complementary exhibition, at the museum, showed something of the life of the Singer family in Frome. *Casting the World* illustrated some of the range of the work that the Singer factory undertook. The Conservation Project is now revealing more detail.

Kim Bowden working on the collection

The negatives are just a small part of the archive that the factory made of their work. We have around 3000 but it is thought that there may have been at least three times that amount. In the 1970s the Singer factory wanted to sell Conigar House which was being used as office space. The attic of the old office building had started to be cleared out in preparation for the move. Thousands of large format glass negatives were being chucked into a skip. The disturbing noise created, raised the curiosity of employee Steve Francis. He recognised the value of the negatives and persuaded the men to stop and take what negatives were left to the museum just across the other side of the river from the factory. Steve worked at the Singer factory all his working life and is now one of the volunteers helping to conserve the negatives.

Being made of glass the negatives are inherently delicate and many of the slides are cracked or have pieces missing. What we are really doing is cleaning off the years of dirt and grime from the glass side of the negative. The photographic emulsion on one side can get damaged from dirt, damp and scratching. In extreme cases the emulsion can come away from the glass plate and be lost. Sarah Allen a Frome based photographic conservator conserved the images that were needed for the exhibition in 2019. She has also trained all those working on the project and given us simple but rigorous rules to make sure we can carefully clean the negatives to minimize future damage. Obviously, none of us are experts but we have gained skills. After gently brushing dirt and dust from the negative the most important task is to identify the glass side of the negative... if we cleaned the emulsion side the image would deteriorate or be destroyed.

Once cleaned, rewrapped in acid free paper and scanned, the record of the work of the factory will be seen online as part of the museum database. This unique collection illustrates just some

of the stunning designs and skills of the Singer's work force. The company's reputation was valued across the world.
What have we discovered while conserving the negatives?

The Singer factory seemingly took photos of most if not all of the items it produced. Some record the factory's work and others were used in sales or exhibition catalogues. There are even some images of intricate jewellery and delicate drinking glasses collected by J W Singer on his journeys to Europe.

One question that has intrigued us, as we cleaned the negatives, is who took these thousands of images? Did the factory have an in-house photographer? Clearly someone was taking images not only to promote the huge range of items being produced. There are the fascinating images of workers in the factory sheds and images of unfinished items. We have found a few clues. Scratched in the corner of some of the negatives are the initials JH. Joseph Humphrey was the photographer who took over the Van Dyck Studios on North Parade in 1889. Though there were several photographers working in Frome at the time and it seems likely that he was the one employed by Singer. It's doubtful that he was the only photographer but as yet we have no evidence of others.

Sue Bucklow knows the images best and has shown us, through her book something of the range of work J W Singer produced especially the cast sculptures. However, the majority of the negatives that we have are of lights, domestic, ecclesiastic and commercial. Some images show one off commissioned lights, for example the electroliers (electric chandeliers) that you can still see in Westminster Cathedral or Bristol Museum and Cardiff City Hall. There are also two stunning images of the electrolier that the Singer factory designed and made for the Pump Rooms in Bath.

Unfortunately, these were replaced in 1959 with the Spanish cut-glass chandeliers that you see today. There are probably many more examples of items made in the Singer factory but they are not credited. When I visited St David's Cathedral recently I saw lighting so similar to the ones we have seen in the collection but to date I haven't heard if they can be verified as being made in Frome. If you visit any heritage property it's always worth asking about the metal fittings such as lighting. If you can, take a photo and we can maybe match it with ones in the collection.

An image from the Singer Collection of negatives showing the mould of one panel for the Scott Memorial that was cast in the Singer factory. The image was digitally coloured by Matt Neilson a year 12 student at Frome College as part of his photography course. With kind thanks to Emma Knibbs Head of Art at the College for collaborating with the museum on this project.

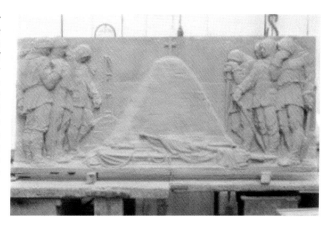

Recently we have come across a sequence of negatives that shows different domestic lights. In each slide the same glass shade is displayed on different metalwork fittings. Clearly the factory was creating different lights through buying in the glass shades and photographing them with a range of different fittings, showing options that retailers could order. In the future we hope that these negatives can be more widely known to show the high quality and variety of the work undertaken at the Singer factory in Frome. It will take some time to scan all the negatives but a selection will soon be available to see online through the Museum website. I believe that there is more to discover by looking in detail at the images. To this end I hope the MA course on Heritage Management at Bath Spa University might have a student interested in using the images as research project for their degree.

Last November I shared some of the digital negatives with the photographic department of Frome College. The students used these to practise digitally adding colour to the images. Hopefully this connection to the College will continue. Local primary schools could use the images of the factory workers and the statues of Boudicca, Queen Victoria or the lions maybe to get to know something of the heritage of the town.

This project has been made possible due primarily to the support of Frome Heritage Museum and the sale of the book *Casting the World*. The author Sue Bucklow generously donated all money raised from the sale to the conservation project. Additionally, an Arts Council grant was successfully applied for from the Small Grant, Big Improvement programme organised by South West museum development.

EDWARD COCKEY'S FORGOTTEN IRON WORKS

John Millns

Thomas Bunn (1767-1853), a wealthy local gentleman and patron of architecture and civic design, owned various properties in the town including the 1793 Longleat lease for a tenement on Golden Knoll adjoining two closes of meadow earlier in the tenure of his late father. The the early 19th-century Cruse tithe map illustrates 'Bunn's Grounds' of approximately nine acres divided into tithed plots numbered 761 to 767 and 773 laid out as allotment gardens occupied by various local tenants.[1] Bunn's extensive grounds fronted four-hundred feet of the carriageway known as 'Behind Town' renamed Christchurch Street by 1830 and eventually Christchurch Street West.

'Bunn's Grounds' shown outlined in red on the tithe map of 1813 and a detail from the 1840 survey confirm the location of Edward Cockey's group of rented plots behind Christchurch Street. Bunn's cottages and gardens on Golden Knoll are seen on both maps.
1840 Tithe Maps: Frome Heritage Museum

From about 1838, one of Bunn's main tenants was Frome's renowned iron-founder and engineer Edward Cockey (1781-1860). His occupation of the six tithed plots 762 to 767 were later renumbered in the later survey of 1840 as plots 179 to 184 with Cockey's timber yard and sheds occupying plot 186 behind Bunn's cottages. The iron-founder continued to rent these plots totalling about 1.6-acres and after 1846 they added about half Bunn's adjoining 5 acres of former meadow 761, including Will Harold's vacated coachmaker's workshops and yards stretching as far as the infant school built earlier on Bunn's land 'gifted' to Christ Church.

1840 Tithe		Owner	Occupier					Acreage	Tithe 1813		
179	BUNN	Thomas	COCKEY	Edward	BATH Lifehold	Garden	Garden	0:0:25	21	19	
180	BUNN	Thomas	COCKEY	Edward	BATH Lifehold	Garden	Garden	0:2:10	21	20	
181	BUNN	Thomas	COCKEY	Edward	BATH Lifehold	Garden	Garden	0:0:26	21	21	763
182	BUNN	Thomas	COCKEY	Edward	BATH Lifehold	Garden	Garden	0:0:21	21	22	764
183	BUNN	Thomas	COCKEY	Edward	BATH Lifehold	Garden	Garden	0:0:11	21	23	765
184	BUNN	Thomas	COCKEY	Edward	BATH Lifehold	Garden	Garden	0:0:31	21	24	766
188	MOON	Joseph	MOON	Joseph	BATH lifehold	House & Garden	Homestead	0:1:33	68	1	773
186	BUNN	Thomas	COCKEY	Edward	BATH Lifehold	Timber Yard & Sheds	Yard &c	0:1:15	21	25	767
187	BUNN	Thomas	BROWN	Henry	BATH Lifehold	House & Premises	Homestead	0:1:24	21	13	768

The 1840 Cruse tithe survey confirms Edward Cockey's occupation of seven plots with corresponding 1813 tithes listed in the last column. Transcription: Frome Historical Research Group

Thomas Bunn's dream had always been to build a range of public buildings fronting his grounds and in 1846 he commissioned the notable Bath architect Edward Davis to draw up plans. Within a month Davis had produced 'beautiful working drawings' for 'a new front towards the street of about four-hundred feet' in an 'improved Grecian' style of architecture stretching between the two entrances to Bunn's grounds recently marked by the architect's ornamental gate piers completed that year.[3] Davis also produced similar 'Grecian designs' for buildings fronting Golden Knoll gardens of about two-hundred feet.[3] However, both ambitious schemes' financial backing failed to materialise at the time, partly due to Bunn's long term illness and the death of his architect.[3] Following Edward Davis's early death in 1852, it fell to his nephew, former pupil and architect Charles E Davis to continue running the Davis architectural practice in Bath while awaiting further instructions to proceed.[10]

Edward Cockey. Will Harold and Will Brown continued to pay rent for their trade workshops and yards occupying about half of Bunn's grounds behind Christchurch Street by 1846. The rate book's references 94 to 97 correlate with notations seen in Maitland & Dixon's rate survey of 1838 for their plots.
Parish Rate Book: Church of St John the Baptist, Frome

Thomas Bunn died in 1853 aged 86. His lifehold tenament on Golden Knoll adjoining his grounds behind Christchurch Street were transferred to his sister Jane Bunn (1769-1862), the remaining life on the 1793 lease, who had agreed to carry on her brother's life's work for the benefit of the people of his native town.[3] Within two years, the young Charles Davis received approvals to proceed with drawing up plans for Frome's police station fronting the street – the first part of Bunn's dream for a terrace of public buildings to be realised. The grand building, designed by Charles E Davis and completed in 1857,[4] was sited next to the entrance to Golden Knoll, where in the summer of 1858 a disastrous fire burnt down three of Bunn's thatched-roofed cottages and damaged others nearby, a timber yard and a 'building' still rented by Edward Cockey.[11 and 12] Later that year, with no natural heirs and approaching 90, Jane Bunn surrendered the lease for the site and adjoining grounds to Lord Bath which included the plots occupied by Bunn's tenants.[12] The Golden Knoll site and plot 186 was bought by the Methodists and about 4-acres of Bunn's former grounds were acquired by the iron-founders including plots 179 to 184 and Harold's adjoining workshops and yards backing onto the Infant School as seen in the later OS survey.

Edward Cockey and Son's workforce more than doubled from 76 men and boys as noted in the family's 1851 census to 166 men and boys confirmed in their 1861 census return which suggests they had increased production and extended their works on Bunn's grounds during the decade.[5] Over the next twenty-five years, the large open site with spacious yards, metalworking shops and sheds, a heavy lifting crane, two weighing machines and a smithy would have enabled Cockey's to develop the range and scale of manufactured iron-work including 'the construction of large boilers and gasometers'[6] alongside the continued production of gas from their Welshmill works and casting traditional gas lighting columns and iron street furniture from the family's well-known foundry tucked away behind 10-15 Bath Street.

In the years following Edward Cockey's death in 1860 aged 79, two of his thirteen children, Henry Cockey (1811-1891) and Francis Christopher Cockey (1815-1888), listed as Engineers, Iron-Founders and Partners at E Cockey and Sons in 1861, were still living at the family home with sisters Maria (1818-1915), Mary Ann (1824-1902) and two general servants at 24 Bath Street built between The Wheat Sheaves Tavern and 1 Market Place.[5] The three-story house, completed about 1823 for Edward and his wife Elizabeth (nee Hagley 1787-1846), replaced their earlier home in the Market Place demolished to make way for the new road.[5 and 9]

By 1871, the two brothers and sisters had moved with their domestics to a fine house with large gardens known as South Hill House built in 1868[7] at 23 Christchurch Street West between The Malthouse and Stoke House at 24.[5] The four unmarried siblings lived at South Hill for many years until it was eventually sold in 1897.[7] Their younger brother George Cockey (1821-1896), a Gas Fitter and Engineer lived with his wife, a young engineering pupil boarder, a bank clerk and servant in residence on Nunney Lane, while Edmund Cockey MD (1817-1907), a Surgeon and Medical Practitioner in the town, lived with his family firstly at 4 South Parade and later next to his siblings at Stoke House before moving the short distance beyond the Fire Engine House to West Lodge at 5 Christchurch Street West.[5]

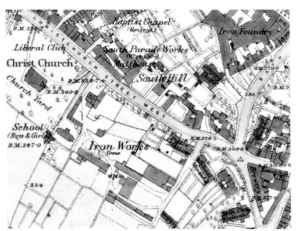

South Hill House with its extensive gardens and tennis lawn provided the perfect location for the Cockey brothers and sisters as it backed onto their Iron Foundry behind Bath Street while the front overlooked their Iron Works across Christchurch Street West partially screened by the

Detail from the 1885 OS survey showing Cockey's South Hill House and gardens overlooking their 4-acre Iron Works site behind Christchurch Street West with its main entrance widened in 1846 adjoining Christ Church School's long gated carriageway built on Bunn's land in 1843. OS Map: National Library of Scotland

Police Station and a walled plantation of trees with steps from the street to their works on higher ground. The colour-coded OS survey of 1885 shows Cockey's Iron Works' buildings mostly unoccupied by that time other than the smithy suggesting manufacturing from behind Christchurch Street West had already transferred to Cockey's Garston Lane site next to the east-west Frome-Radstock GWR mineral line with its rail link to Bristol. Following Francis Christopher Cockey's death in 1888 and Henry's in 1891 at the age of 79, the final transfer of production from their Bath Street Foundry two years later completed the company's relocation to the Garston site and marked the beginning of the next phase of development for Edward Cockey and Sons Ltd.[8]

South Hill House at 23 Christ Church Street West the home of the four Cockey siblings between 1868-1897. The photograph dated 1909 shows the south-east elevation with James Short's grandaughter standing on the lawn. James founded the carriage works and showrooms adjoining the house where his family lived between 1897 and 1909.[7] The house and buildings were demolished shortly after the First World War to make way for Frome's War Memorial Hall. Photo: Frome Heritage Museum

Less then forty-years after Thomas Bunn's death in 1853, the police station designed in the fashionable Gothic style of the time by the twenty-nine-year old Bath architect Charles Edward Davis* opened in 1857. Wesley Villas and the school buildings built on Golden Knoll designed in a similar Gothic style by the young Bath architect William John Wilcox opened in 1863 and replaced Bunn's cottages;[11] the town's Public Offices by architects Halliday & Anderson in an Italian Renaissance style opened in 1892,[4] and the late Victorian villas including a vicarage built in stone with gabled terracotta tiled roofs and canted bay windows overlooking the town, went some way to achieving Bunn's earlier vision of building a six-hundred feet terrace of fine public buildings and dwellings fronting his Golden Knoll gardens and grounds behind Christchurch Street West to rival the architecture in Bath.

*In 1862 Charles E Davis was appointed City Architect and Surveyor of Bath which he held for the next forty years alongside running the Davis private practice at 3 Westgate Buildings, Bath.[10] while his contempory William J Wilcox of the Wilson and Wilcox practice in Bath was eventually appointed Somerset County Architect.[11]

Today, the Braeside Works' former site and Nunney Garage occupy a large part of Cockey's former iron works site hidden behind the old police station and Victorian villas, the Memorial Theatre complex occupies the former South Hill House and gardens site, while the recently demolished malthouse building has been replaced by apartments linked to the South Parade Works' redevelopment.

Detail from the 1902 OS revisions confirm Frome's Public Offices, the newly built Victorian Villas and Park Road cut through the former Iron Works to access Victoria Park opened in 1887 – the Queen's Golden Jublee year. The School of Science and Art were also built on Bunn's former grounds along with part of Victoria Hospital by 1901. Victoria Diamond Jubilee Swimming and Slipper Baths opened in 1897 converted from Cockey's former Bath Street Foundry.
OS Map: National Library of Scotland

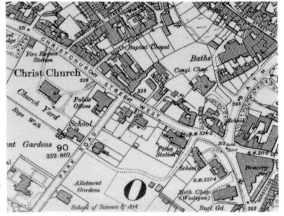

The Public Offices building occupied by Frome's Town Hall stands directly over the former site of Christchurch School's gates and main entrance to the former iron works both demolished in 1891 along with a pair of Bunn's gate piers.[3] One of the damaged piers was discovered in a local garden in 2002, restored and resited in front of the recently refurbished Town Hall some four-hundred feet from the remaining original pier designed by Edward Davis in 1846 and now grade II listed. It stands as a tribute to Thomas Bunn on the corner of Wesley Close between the grade II old police station and the grade II Wesley Buildings on Golden Knoll.

Although not built in his preferred 'improved Grecian' style of architecture, Bunn's inspired vision for a terrace of fine public buildings and dwellings fronting his former grounds was finally realised before the end of the 19th-century. The impressive six-hundred feet terrace stretching from Wesley Buildings to the Town Hall continues to enjoy a commanding presence within the street's conservation area of special architectural interest, while the former site of Edward Cockey and Sons' iron works, almost forgotten for over a century, should now be celebrated and added to Frome's Heritage and Industrial Trails.

References

1   1813 Cruse Survey of the Parish of Frome, www.gomezsmart.myzen.co.uk
2   Tithe Apportionments for the Parish of Frome, 1840, www.gomezsmart.myzen.co.uk
3   *The Diary of Thomas Bunn of Frome*, published by FSLS, edited by Derek Gill, 2003
4   Frome's former Police Station and Public Offices, www.historicengland.org.uk
5   UK Census Records for 1851 to 1891, https://www.ancestry.co.uk/
6   Edward Cockey and Sons, *Graces Guide to British Industrial History*, www.gracesguide.co.uk
7   South Hill House, Frome www.historicengland.org.uk
8   Cockey Families, www.gomezsmart.myzen.co.uk
9   *The Buildings of Frome*, Rodney D Goodall, FSLS, 2005
10   *Edward Davis, 19th Century Bath Architect*, Michael Forsyth, and
        Charles E Davis Bath Architect, Barry Cunliffe, History of Bath Research Group, on-line
11   *Wesleyan Buildings and the Architect William J Wilcox,* Volume 18, 2015, FSLS
12   1793 Longleat lease extract with attached notes and letters, www.gomezsmart.myzen.co.uk

Also,   Edward Cockey, www.wikipedia.org
         The Cockey Family, www.geni.com
         The Cockey Story Exhibition, Frome Museum and Cockey files, Sue Latham, 2021

Many thanks to St John the Baptist Church, Frome Historical Research Group and Frome Museum for access to their archives.

THE NAME OF FROME: What Happened to the other 'O'?

Lisa Kenwright

As a guide of historical walks around Frome, I am often impressed with the level of knowledge many of the local inhabitants have about their own town and how many can tell you what 'Frome' means. I recently led a walk for 30 seven-year-olds and all of them were able to shout out 'fair and brisk' when asked about the origins of the town's name. Many are also aware that the name at one time was spelled as *Froome* and so one of the most frequent questions I am asked is 'What happened to the other 'o'? This article is my attempt to answer that question. However, to do that, we first have to ask, 'where did the second 'o' come from in the first place?'

My degree, many years ago now, was in linguistics and while I was never an expert in either philology (the study of language in oral and written historical sources) or etymology (the study of the history of words) I knew enough to have the beginnings of a hypothesis. During lockdown I finally got the time to look into this question in more depth and I did a great deal of research online. As I was unable to access the original documents and lack the specialist knowledge needed to sort out the complex issues, I still cannot answer either of these questions with certainty, but what follows could be seen as an interim report on what I have so far. Margaret Gelling, the late-twentieth-century expert in the study of English place-names, gives a strong warning against 'amateurs' working in this area (Gelling 1988 pp12-13). However, she also says that local historians might be useful in gathering local data (ibid pp15-16). This is my attempt to do the latter while trying not to be too amateurish.

My focus here is on how the name has changed since the Saxon settlement of the area in the seventh century. The exact form and pronunciation of the original Brittonic name for the river will have affected how the Saxons heard the word, and therefore how they said and wrote it when they adopted it for their new settlement. However, the written evidence that we have dates from the time of St Aldhelm onwards so that is what I have used to track the changes over time. I have therefore side-stepped the issue of its original meaning and form in the post-Roman era and concentrated on the primary element of the name. While the changing series of secondary names from *Braunche* to *Vallis* to *Selwood* and the many different spellings thereof is fascinating in its own right, reasons of time and space mean it will have to be put aside for another day.

My tentative hypothesis, based on my incomplete linguistic knowledge, was that originally the name of the town was pronounced by the Saxon inhabitants with a long vowel roughly akin to the initial vowel sound in the Modern English word 'so' and gradually changed to the modern version through the process of the Great Vowel Shift - the change in the pronunciation of certain English vowels that occurred from around the 14th to the 16th centuries. I assumed this was then reflected by a universal change in the spelling to *Froome* around the 14th or 15th century. I was less clear as to when and why it might have changed back but speculated that it was led by Victorian antiquarians discovering the original spelling and deliberately changing it, as happened in the nearby village of Rode, once *Road*. When I looked at the evidence it was not so simple. I have not been able to draw any definite conclusions about how the name was originally pronounced or how it changed over time. The change in spelling, though easier to track given the abundance of printed material from the 17th century onwards, is also not as clear cut as I hoped. I have disproved at least part of my original hypothesis in the process of researching the various linguistic factors that might be involved in tracking a name over such a long period. I have also brought together in one place information on the available early spellings which could provide the basis for further study.

A Rough and Ready Introduction to IPA and the Delights of Phonology

The story of the name of the town of Frome spans the history of the English language from Old English (locally that means from arrival of the West Saxons in the 7th century up to roughly the Norman Conquest) through Middle English (to around 1500) and Modern English (from 1500 to now). These dates are approximate and the changes from one to the next would have been gradual so would not have been that obvious to contemporary speakers beyond the familiar 'youngsters today don't speak properly....'. Looking back across 13 centuries we are essentially trying to understand foreign languages, albeit ones that contain the roots of our own everyday speech, each with very different systems of encoding meaning onto sound and of mapping those sounds onto speech. To discuss the development of a word through time we have to find a way through the difficulties of different orthographies to be able to show how a word is pronounced. The International Phonetic Alphabet (IPA) is the usual method used by linguists and more recent editions of the OED though most dictionaries will use their own respelling scheme to demonstrate how a word should be said. These various other schemes have limitations, not least that many English speakers, myself included, do not speak Received Pronunciation (RP, supposedly standard English but that is a long discussion for a different publication) so do not share the baseline pronunciation. The helpful note 'rhymes with aunt not ant' does not help speakers who say 'aunt' exactly the same as 'ant'. There are various websites that give an overview of the values of each symbol in IPA including a useful page at Wikipedia to get you started which has the advantage of being linked to sound files to avoid the limitations of written explanations, though of course the usual warnings of using that site apply!

The study of the production and perception of sounds used in human language is called 'phonetics'. 'Phonology' is the study of a sound within a specific system, that is a particular language. It is of course impossible to go into a full description of IPA and the values of different signs here, hopefully I will explain what you need to know as I go through.

In phonology, a symbol is assigned the value of a sound, called a 'phoneme'. Unlike in writing, the value of each symbol is constant within the phonology of that language. Phonemes are written within slashes to demonstrate the theoretical pronunciation (rather than the actual transcription of what someone said), usually of a standard speaker. For example, the symbol /u:/ represents the vowel in the modern RP pronunciation of Frome (and for the benefit of non-locals, it rhymes with 'room') but it is approximate, not everyone will say it quite the same. A colon after the vowel symbol shows that it is a relatively long vowel. The vowel in Frome is longer than for example the sound in 'ship', a short vowel in RP (but not in Old English and some modern dialects).

The single letter representing a vowel, as in /u/, tells us that it is a pure vowel or a monophthong rather than a diphthong. In the former the vowel is said without moving the tongue, in the latter the tongue glides between two positions. If you can't tell which is which, try overextending the vowel in question - most people can say the vowel in Frome till their breath runs out and would probably write it something along the lines of 'oooooooo'. Now try the written vowels you learned at school. They are diphthongs for most speakers of British English dialects. The symbol for the name of 'o', as in 'home', is /əʊ/, the two symbols giving us the start and end points of the phoneme. Try to extend that sound and you will become aware of the need to move your mouth to complete the vowel. This particular phoneme is relevant to us as it represents the pronunciation of 'Frome' most often attempted by those not in the know. It is also the sound in 'so' mentioned in the introduction, but in Old English it would not be a diphthong.

Technically, Old English and Modern English are treated as different languages so should be studied using two different phonologies. This means that the symbols as /u:/ actually might have different values at different points in our timeline but hopefully the massive simplification will show enough to be of use. I have adopted the usual convention of putting older versions of words and place-names in italics, NE words are in single quotes. I have therefore used *Frome* for the OE and ME mentions of the name and 'Frome' for the modern one.

As we have no access to native speakers of the earlier stages of English for obvious reasons, we cannot record and transcribe actual speech to discover the true pronunciation of a word at a given point. There has been a great deal of study by experts over nearly a century and there is a lot of information available on how people would [likely] have said certain sounds at different points. One of the pieces of evidence used is the way that the written word was spelled. Until around the 1600s people wrote what they heard regardless of the actual pronunciation, rather than using a standard spelling as we do today.

We would write the word 'look' the same, whether it was being said by someone from Liverpool or someone from London and whether we ourselves were from London or Liverpool. A transcription of the pronunciation using IPA however would show the differences. Throughout the Medieval period, the spelling of a word would be more likely to reflect that different pronunciation as there was no standardisation, which only began to develop from the 16th century onwards and a clear-cut distinction between correct' and incorrect' did not develop until the eighteenth century (Crystal p223). However, the written evidence is further complicated because speakers of different dialects would also likely give different values (pronunciations) to the written letters they were using.

How the sounds of a spoken language are mapped onto written symbols, essentially letters or groups of letters, is called the 'orthography' of a language. The same letters will have different values in different orthographies. A full study of how the name of this town has been said through history would involve the phonologies and orthographies of [Medieval] Latin, Old English (OE), Middle English (ME) and Modern English (NE) as well as the phonology of Brittonic, the language of the Romano-British people who originally named the river but didn't leave us many written examples of their writing. Each of those languages would also have regional differences as well as changes over time within the greater time period, in the case of OE and ME.

Finally, for the purposes of spoken language, a vowel is a phoneme where the sound is shaped by the tongue and lips, but not impeded as in a consonant. In spoken Modern English there are over a dozen pure vowels and around seven diphthongs, depending on dialect. Although many consonants and their representation in writing have also changed since the time of OE, those in our name of interest have not changed noticeably so we will largely be dealing with vowels. So to summarise, the average 'correct' pronunciation of the whole name 'Frome' in Modern English would be written /fruːm/ in IPA. The pronunciation most likely attempted by those not in the know, who have been fooled by the spelling to rhyme it with 'home', would be written as /frəʊm/.

Great Vowel Shift

When I began looking into the history of the Frome name I was rather startled to realise that some local historians believed it had not changed pronunciation over the course of its known 1300 years of history. It is unusual to come across a name that has kept the same written form from ME, however that does not mean it had the same pronunciation throughout its history. As I have already pointed out, orthography has changed and 'o' no longer has the same set of possible values in NE it once had in OE and ME. One reason why such consistency of pronunciation over 13 centuries is unlikely is the marvellously named Great Vowel Shift (GVS).

This is the term for the series of changes in pronunciation of vowels, particularly the stressed long vowels, which occurred between around 1300 and 1700. The term was first coined by Otto Jespersen (1860–1943), a Danish linguist. An example would be the OE word *tūn* (/tu:n/ for those who are getting the hang of IPA) meaning 'enclosure' which changed form and meaning through several stages to became the modern word 'town' (/taʊn/). A transitional form can be found on the end of many local place names '-ton'. These changes did not occur simultaneously across the country – 'town', 'house' or 'out' in some northern English and Scots dialects are still said with the /u:/ as they would have been in OE, rather than as the NE (/taʊn/, /haʊse/ or /aʊt/.

Because the standardisation of English spellings started part way through this period of change (15th to 16th century) the spellings for many words 'froze' at the moment before they changed pronunciation. Thus, the GVS is believed to be the one of the main sources of the irregular, non-phonetic and occasionally downright bizarre spellings of written Modern English.

What caused these changes is a matter of a great deal of debate if not actual argument, however there is large agreement on the basic patterns of change. Take the *tūn* to 'town' shift mentioned above. Apart from the different pattern in the north-east, words with this same vowel mostly changed the same way, in several phases, though not necessarily at the same time. This is an incredibly complex area and I do not claim to be expert enough to state with any certainty how the GVS affected the pronunciation of our town's name. However, I did find some interesting parallels that are suggestive. Following the pattern of the series just mentioned, if 'Frome' had originally been said /fru:m/ you might expect it to now be pronounced to rhyme with modern 'town' ie with the diphthong /aʊ/ and have a spelling with 'u' or 'w'.

There is a counter-example, however. The NE word 'room' (/ru:m/) would seem to have kept the same pronunciation without changing with the other long vowels, although its meaning has shifted slightly. This was originally reflected in the OE spelling of the word as *rum* and the ME *roum* . If 'Frome' was originally pronounced as it is now, we might expect to find early spellings such as **Frum* (the asterix denotes a non-existent or theoretical form).

The pattern of changes I suggest might fit this case is that demonstrated by OE *mōna* /mo:na/ which became our modern 'moon' /mu:n/. The macron over the 'o' in the OE is a modern convention to show a long vowel. The OE vowel does not exist in most modern English varieties but as stated earlier, the first part of the diphthong in 'doe' or 'so' is close. (Crystal p 251-2).

The OE pronunciation of *Frome* is also possibly complicated by the nasal consonant 'm' which can affect how the preceding vowel is pronounced particularly the vowel /ɑ/ (closest to the vowel in modern word 'palm' which even *I* say with the vowel of RP 'aunt') which can move closer to /ɒ/ or the sound in 'lot' and might be spelled with an 'o' to prove it. Does that affect the word we are looking at? Well possibly if the original Brittonic word was *Frama* but now we are really beyond the lands I can possibly know. Another piece of evidence is the existence of the form Frampton for several settlements on the other rivers Frome, formed from the river name + *tūn*. Again more research is needed and we need to look at the available evidence.

Written Examples

I looked for all the sources I could for the early mentions of the name. Michael McGarvie's books (2000, 2013) were an invaluable signpost for places to look but I also used the relevant entries in Ekwall (1977). I mostly accessed transcriptions and copies of original documents via online databases including British History Online for the Calendar of the Close Rolls, Inquisitions Post Mortem, the Journal of the House of Lords, the Journal of the House of Commons and other documents; the online catalogue of the Somerset Records Office; the British Newspaper Archive; the Electronic Sawyer (a database of Saxon charters) and the British Library's electronic collection. I am not claiming that this is exhaustive and I am well aware of the limitations of using secondary sources and transcriptions for something so dependent on the precise spelling of ancient and hard to read documents as the history of a place-name. It is however a start and unfortunately all that could be achieved during lockdown when all records offices were closed to visitors.

Old English

The earliest mention of the town in writing that I could find is in McGarvie (2000), quoting a boundary charter which I could not access directly: '*thanen on Fromesetting hagen*' from 694 CE which he translates as 'the dwellers around Frome'. OE was an inflected language - words changed ending according to gender, case and number in sentences and compound words which can lead to misleading interpretations.

The earliest mention of the town proper is often given as a letter of 701 CE from Pope Sergius to St Aldhelm granting certain rights to his monastery in the town. This actually references the river, not the town itself, and was the source of confusion as various sources quote this as both *From* and *Frome*. This document has been regarded as dubious and possibly a medieval forgery on the part of the monks of Malmesbury. The original is no longer extant and as is common for documents of this age, only exists in copies. There are in fact two versions both quoted in Birch (1885). One is from William of Malmesbury and is in Latin. I have only seen the printed version in Birch (pp152-4) where the town is named as *From*. The other is an OE translation of the latter. A printed transcription can be found in Birch (pp 154-6) but the original is available at the British Library online collection and consists of an 11th-century insertion in a 10th-century gospel. It is very damaged (from the famous Cotton fire) but refers to the town as *Fron* as quoted in Birch.

These two documents (assuming they are copies of a genuine 701 CE original) illustrate the complexity of the task. Is that *Fron* a reflection of the actual spelling and pronunciation of the 7th century, the 11th century, or simply a mistake in copying? The Latin document on the other hand is a perfect example of why the specific language orthography matters. Most modern English speakers would read *From* as identical to our modern preposition 'from', with the NE sound /ɒ/ also in the word 'hot'. In Latin, however, the grapheme 'o' is usually deemed to have two possible values, long and short. This is not my area at all but online crib sheets suggest /ɔ/ as the value for the short vowel (so a short version of the vowel in 'law') and /oː/ for the long vowel, so similar to the OE long vowel we met in the previous section.

After that there is a charter by St Aldhelm in 705, possibly dubious, available at the Electronic Sawyer which gives *Froom*, followed by two versions of the Anglo-Saxon Chronicle, A and F, which mention the death of Eadred in CE 955 at *Frome*. The Parker Chronicle or A is the oldest, begun in the late 9th century and therefore possibly containing contemporaneous text in 955. It is believed to have originated in Wessex, possibly Winchester. The F Chronicle is dated to the late 11th or early 12th century so is presumably a copy of an earlier version, possibly the Parker Chronicle. These can also be found in the British Library online archive.

Thus, either the 705 charter or the Parker Chronicle are probably the earliest written examples of the name of the town, one of which gives *Frome* and one *Froom*. I cannot therefore draw any definite conclusions about the early Saxon pronunciation of the name except that none of the various spellings so far seem to support the possibility it was said /fruːm/ in the modern manner. Another possible factor in the variety of spellings, besides differences in pronunciation and orthography, is the aforementioned inflection of both OE and Latin. In OE, place-names are often written in the dative which will also affect both the pronunciation and spelling.

Middle English Period

The Middle English period, when our language underwent huge changes, is usually deemed to begin with the Norman Conquest, however it should be remembered that while that momentous event was probably the trigger for many of the developments in English, the changes themselves would have taken some time to show. The Domesday survey of 1088 is the next major piece of evidence but do bear in mind that it was written in Latin by Norman clerks. There are two mentions of the town, both given as *Frome*.

The next mention was an Inquisition Post Mortem, for Joan Braunche of 1279 at British History Online (BHO) where I also searched the Close Calendar Rolls. This revealed many mentions of the town and from that document of 1279 to 1540, every one of them spelled the name of this town as *Frome*, including the names of the various other settlements with the same name. There are problems here too of course. Not one of these documents could be seen in the original text. The majority were carefully transcribed to preserve original spellings but the 'originals' are often Victorian transcriptions of the actual originals. Did they preserve the true contemporary spelling? While this question should be born in mind, the other names associated with Frome do change during this period: *Braunche* and *Branche*, often in the same document; *Valeys* and *Valeyse* for Vallis; *Selewode* and *Selwode*, not to mention the variety of spellings of other nearby settlements such as Rodden and Marston Bigot.

To check if there were regional differences, I also searched at the South West Heritage Trust online Somerset Archive Catalogue and from the 13th century to well into the 17th, the result was the same. Here there is even more need for caution, for I was searching catalogue entries which are largely summaries of the documents and it is unclear how accurately they have followed the original spelling, although they do show a change in some cases in the later period and some alternative spellings of local settlements are shown. The sheer volume of documents available all using the spelling *Frome* suggests this was the usual spelling into the Early Modern English period with an interesting lack of any transitional forms.

Modern English Period

It is only in the Modern English period I began to come across that elusive second 'o'. At BHO I found the earliest occurrence in the Journal of the House of Lords of 1641 on Sir J. Thynn's Bill, 'An Act for disforesting of certain Lands of Sir *James Thynne's*, Knight, Parcel of the Forest of *Zelwood*, alias *Froome Selwood*, in the County of *Somersett'*. The same collection of papers has several such mentions through the 1640s, one from 1656 and on to the 1760s. However, this overlaps with three mentions of *Frome Selwood* in the State Papers of the Interregnum, 1654 to 1656. From this point this database presents mostly the spelling of *Froome* or *Froom* for all the settlements and rivers of the same name into the nineteenth century with occasional reversions to Frome, particularly from around 1820, often in the same documents that also have *Froome*.

There is a list of members of the University of Oxford 1500 to 1714, the *Alumni Oxonienses,* which gives an interesting overview as, though written itself in 1891, presumably it was taken from contemporary records. Amongst others, Walter Collins (Colyns) was vicar of *Frome Selwood* in 1529; Thomas Higgons (sic) was vicar of *Frome Selwood* in 1597 to 1606; Joseph Ivileafe of *Frome Selwood* matriculated in 1665; Thomas Hill of *Froom* is mentioned in 1671; Francis Langworth of *Frome* matriculated in 1681, then it is *Froom* or *Froome* from 1685 to 1714.

In the Somerset records however we see a different pattern, with only around 20 examples of the *Froome* spelling even after its first appearance in a bond in 1594, with a handful of *Froom* mentions referring to this town, the rest are a personal name. The latest such mention is Rev. Bennett's book *The Old Church of St John Baptist, Froome Selwood* of 1888. Search on 'Frome' for the same period of 1594 to 1888 and you get nearly 4000 hits. Many will not be relevant but the difference in numbers is suggestive. I also searched at the British Newspaper Archive but realised the data was too complicated to be collated in time for this paper. I suspect more careful analysis may find that local sources favour the older form. Searching *The Frome Times* for *Froome* gets 300 results from the mid-19th century to 1899 but *Frome* over 22,000 times in the same period.

More work would need to be done here.

Conclusions

As I said at the beginning I cannot claim to have answered my questions about the spelling of Frome or even be certain on how it developed from its earliest use. At the very least I hope I have demonstrated the number of disparate elements that would have to be considered in any attempt to trace the history of even such a deceptively simple name as Frome.

I would suggest that the evidence points to the following:

The paucity of contemporaneous written evidence from the OE period and the differences in the material we do have means it is hard to state what the Saxon pronunciation would have been. However, it seems unlikely to have been the modern /fru:m/ simply because in the variety of spelling in those sources none of them uses a 'u'. The accepted patterns of the Great

Vowel Shift suggest it might have been closer to /froːm/, actually not far from the main 'wrong' pronunciation in our times. Further study, preferably by someone with more expertise in OE, would be required here.

The admittedly faulty examples from the Middle English period suggest that the spelling *Frome* was usual into the Early Modern English period. I realised that I would have to do a lot more reading on this area, particularly the changes early in ME. The written evidence suggests that Frome could well fit the /oː/ to /uː/ pattern under the GVS but the lack of transitional forms seen in other similar words is interesting. Possibly I was looking at the shift the wrong way round, rather than a late change in pronunciation being shown by the extra 'o', the change came early in the ME period and a late change in orthography from ME to NE led to people wanting to add that extra letter. It is also possible that the local pronunciation was different to the 'standard' used in London. The GVS is a specialist subject and more study on the localised patterns of change would be required here.

The spelling *Frome* continued into the modern period and existed in tandem with *Froome* from at least the sixteenth century. At no point does the latter seem to have become completely dominant locally and (possibly misleading) word-searches suggest the former more common by several orders of magnitude though inconsistently, with both spellings used in the same text in some cases. In the Victorian era the second 'o' would appear to be the exception not the rule in printed sources including many locally-printed pamphlets and books. That does not mean that locals didn't use *Froome* in their everyday written communication, however I could find no evidence that the town adopted that spelling officially. A detailed study of local handwritten and printed sources would be needed here - I did not have access to the library and museum resources during the main period of research for this article. I feel I have, at least partially, debunked my own hypothesis here. It does not appear that *Froome* was ever the accepted standard, at least not locally, and it may well have been a matter of personal background or indeed preference.

This brief overview does not really show the full extent of my research and to reach definite conclusions would involve a good deal more. Hopefully one day I will have a chance to continue this study when free time coincides with the ability to travel and visits to record offices are possible.

Bibliography

Anonymous. 10th/11th century. *Cotton MS Otho C I/1 f68.* British Library Online Collection: Accessed 29/9/20
Birch, Walter de Gray. 1885. *Cartularium saxonicum: a collection of charters relating to Anglo-Saxon history.* London: Whiting. Accessed online at the Internet Archive 29/9/20
Crystal, David, The Stories of English, 2004, Penguin Allen Lane
Crystal, David. 2004. *The Stories of English.* London: Allen Lane
Ekwall, Eilert. 1977. *The Concise Oxford Dictionary of English Place-names: Fourth Edition.* Oxford: OUP
Gelling, Margaret. 1988. *Signposts to the Past.* Chichester: Phillimore
McGarvie, Michael. 2000. *Frome Through the Ages: An Anthology in Prose and Verse.* Frome: FSLS
McGarvie: Michael. 2013. *The Book of Frome.* Frome: FSLS
Pollington, Stephen. 2008. *First Steps in Old English.* Swaffham: Anglo-Saxon Books

Online Resources

The British Newspaper Archive https://www.britishnewspaperarchive.co.uk/
The Electronic Sawyer https://esawyer.lib.cam.ac.uk. Accessed 15/12/21
Open Domesday https://opendomesday.org/place/ST7747/frome/ Accessed 20/12/21
South West Heritage Trust Online Somerset Archive Catalogue https://somerset-cat.swheritage.org.uk

FROME IN PRINT

These are some of the most popular and informative books on the town's history obtainable from: Frome Museum, 1 North Parade 01373 454 661. Hunting Raven Books 10 Cheap Street 01373 473 111 or by post from frome-heritage-museum.org postage is charged at cost. A full 42-page regularly updated digital catalogue is also available via the website.

The Book of Frome (5th ed) by Michael McGarvie   £15.00
The definitive history of Frome describing the town from its foundation in around 685 until 2000 covering all aspects of the town many photographs, drawings and maps. 163 pages.

Frome Street and Place Names (4th ed) by Michael McGarvie   £6.00
An erudite and entertaining description of the derivation of the place and street names in Frome. Many of these date from the middle ages or recall the names of householders who lived in the street. 52 pages.

The Historic Inns of Frome (3rd reprint) by Mick Davis & Valerie Pitt £10.00
The history of Frome's pubs past & present from the long-lost Albion in Cheap Street via the ancient Blue Boar the magical Crooked Fish and the elusive Wyredrawers Arms. 180 pages.

Experiences of a 19th Century Gentleman by Derek Gill (ed)   £10.00
The extensive diary of Thomas Bunn, Frome philanthropist who lived from 1767-1853 and initiated many improvements to the town. His diaries range from 1836-1852 and are an absolute mine of information about the town and its characters. 196 pages.

The Buildings of Frome (3rd ed) by Rodney Goodall   £9.00
Rodney Goodall was an architect in Frome for over 40 years. He describes the development of the town with detailed descriptions of Frome's outstanding collection of buildings which he relates to the economic and social history of the town. Fully illustrated. 150 pages.

Frome Heritage Trail   revised edition 2022   £3.00
The trail follows a series of plaques the 1300th anniversary of the founding of Frome in 685AD. The pamphlet guides the reader through the whole of the old town and describes the important buildings in their historical context. The ideal walking guide. 16 pages.

Crime & Punishment in Regency Frome Michael McGarvie (ed) £9.00
The journals of Isaac Gregory, Constable of Frome in 1813-4 and 1817-8 give an original description of how life was lived in the town and the trials and tribulations suffered by the constable in the early part of the 19th century. 63 pages.

The Awful Killing of Sarah Watts by Mick Davis & David Lassman   £12.00
The story of Frome's unsolved murder from 1851.Sarah Watts was raped and murdered while her parents were out at the market. Despite intense enquiries and the trial of four suspects there were no convictions. A detailed examination of the town's Victorian underworld. 257 pages.

Foul Deeds & Suspicious Deaths in Frome. by Mick Davis & David Lassman   £10.00
14 cases from Frome's criminal history including witchcraft, highwayman, murder and madness, suicide and fraud. A cornucopia of criminal delights fully illustrated. 129 pages.

The Butler & Tanner Story   by Dr Lorraine Johnson   £12.00
Tells the story of Butler and Tanner from its foundation by William Langford printing labels for his chemist shop to become the finest colour printer in the country. Charts the slow decline of the company which closed in 2014. many illustrations 133 pages.

Of Mounds & Men   by Mick Davis   £12.00
The prehistoric barrows of the Frome area are described as they appear today and in the early 19c recorded by Rev John Skinner who opened and sketched many of the barrows reproduced for the first time in this book. Many photographs, providing the first guide to prehistoric barrows in North Somerset. Also acts as a guidebook to be taken on visits. 137 pages.

A History of Mells (3rd ed) by Rev FW Cleverdon   £7.50
This village history was originally published in 1974. Cleverdon, who was rector of Mells from 1959-69, used the church records and Horner manuscripts to produce a well-researched history of the village from the middle ages to 1970. Many old photographs. 102 pages.

Frome in the Great War by David Lassman   £12.99
The First World War comes to Frome. Local men experienced action in all the theatres of war that the global conflict encompassed, taking part in numerous battles and campaigns on land and sea; its a civilian population received a special commendation after the war for its efforts throughout. 106 pages.

Frome at War 1939-1945   by David Lassman   £14.99
A comprehensive account of the Frome's war years giving rare insights into the life of the town including its part in the secret underground resistance movement, the influx of GIs and tales of endurance and courage. 222 pages.

Frome Town Hall by Dr Lorraine Johnson   £7.50
A history of the towns administrative centre completed in 1892. It has housed a host of characters throughout its long history and this is the story of how and why it was built and the story of those who worked there with many illustrations. 111 pages.

Villages of the Frome Area: A History by Peter Belham   £4.50
Peter Belham describes the development of the villages close to Frome from the Norman conquest to the end of the 20th century. He explains the influence of their geography on their growth and the importance of Frome as a centre of the region. Illustrated 150 pages.

A Surfeit of Magnificence by Mick Davis   £14.95
The incredible story of Sir Thomas Champneys of Orchardleigh a flamboyant aristocrat who whose incredible debts didn't stop a life of indulgence and entertaining on a lavish scale despite his creditors constantly raiding his magnificent house and sending him to prison for debt on several occasions. 178 pages.

Ordnance Survey map of Central Frome 1886   £10.00
This is to the scale of 1:1000 and covers the nine sheets of central Frome. Supplied folded and opens out to 127×83 cm. It can be supplied flat from the museum if preferred.